GO DEEP

Doris e. Kizinna

GO Deep

SPIRITUAL PRACTICES
FOR YOUTH MINISTRY

CopperHouse

Editor: Ingrid Turnbull
Cover and interior design: Verena Velten
Prepress Production: Chaunda Daigneault
Proofreader: Dianne Greenslade
Photo on cover © iStockphoto.com/Ryan Klos
Photo on spine: © iStockphoto.com/Aleksandr Pakhay
Photos on back cover (top to bottom): © Doris Kizinna, © shutterstock.com/Iko
     © iStockphoto.com/Aleksandr Pakhay, © iStockphoto.com/Clayton Hansen

CopperHouse is an imprint of Wood Lake Publishing, Inc. Wood Lake Publishing
acknowledges the financial support of the Government of Canada, through the Book
Publishing Industry Development Program (BPIDP) for its publishing activities. Wood Lake
Publishing also acknowledges the financial support of the Province of British Columbia
through the Book Publishing Tax Credit.

At Wood Lake Publishing, we practise what we publish, being guided by a concern for fairness, justice, and equal opportunity in all of our relationships with employees and customers. Wood Lake Publishing is an employee-owned company, committed to caring for the environment and all creation. Wood Lake Publishing recycles, reuses, and encourages readers to do the same. Resources are printed on 100% post-consumer recycled paper and more environmentally friendly groundwood papers (newsprint), whenever possible. A percentage of all profit is donated to charitable organizations.

Library and Archives Canada Cataloguing in Publication

Kizinna, Doris E. (Doris Ellen), 1969-
   Go deep : spiritual practices for youth ministry / Doris E. Kizinna.
ISBN 978-1-55145-575-4
   I. Church work with youth. 2. Christian leadership. 3. Spiritual life–Christianity. I. Title.
BV4447.K579 2009   259'.23   C2009-904234-7

Published by CopperHouse
An imprint of Wood Lake Publishing Inc.
485 Beaver Lake Road, Kelowna, BC, Canada, V4V 1S5
www.woodlake.com
250.766.2778

Printing 10 9 8 7 6 5 4 3 2
Printed in Canada

DEDICATION

I dedicate this book to the Source of Life;
the Heart of Heaven and the Heart of Earth,
where we have come from and where we will one day return.
I offer humble thanks for all the blessings.

CONTENTS

acknowledgments

It feels as though everything that I have done in my life until now has prepared me for writing this resource. Through it, I hope to share some of what I have learned about wisdom and creativity with the world. I offer deep thanks to the many people who have influenced my life: teachers, mentors, family, friends, and colleagues.

I extend my heartfelt gratitude to my church – The United Church of Canada. You nurtured me as a child, tended me as a young person, offered me a place of ministry as a young adult, and gave me a vocation. I particularly wish to thank Aldergrove United Church where I grew up and was loved into community; Crescent United Church where I began my life in paid youth ministry; Ryerson United Church where I deepened my ministry with youth for seven years; and B.C. Conference of the United Church of Canada where I fine-tuned my work with youth, young adults, and youth leaders across British Columbia. I want to thank the large network of Youth and Young Adult Ministry in B.C. Conference of The United Church of Canada, which has helped make me a strong leader. I am grateful for the freedom I was given to create and live out community the way I felt called. Thank you.

My thanks go to the youth who have accompanied me over the last 20 years. I have often been astounded by your depth, compassion, creativity, and the light that you all bring to the world. Thank you for allowing me to be part of your lives.

My thanks go to Naramata Centre, where I have had some of my greatest moments in community and leadership. Thank you for providing a safe haven of faith, community, and learning for me and so many others.

Thank you to all those leaders who have helped me develop the practices and given practical assistance. My thanks go especially to Tressa Brotsky, who brought her exceptional creativity and wisdom to many practice experiences.

Thank you to Wood Lake Books for seeing the need for a youth ministry resource with a liberal theology, and for helping me to make it happen. Thanks to Ingrid Turnbull for editing this resource, turning my conversational writing into something literary!

Thank you to Donna Scorer, Tim Scorer, Maya Landell, and Keri Wehlander; colleagues and friends; and my family for your encouragement.

Thanks to Allison Rennie, my soul friend, who planted the idea of the spiritual practices in my being at the beginning. Your leadership and insights are woven throughout this book. I am grateful for your wisdom and your presence in my life.

For all those along this path who have helped me to see the Source of Life alive and at work in my life, thank you.

Doris Kizinna
Naramata, 2009

INTRODUCTION

Below what we think we are
we are something else,
we are almost anything.

~ D.H. Lawrence

I am being and becoming. I am living and learning. I am better off for all that I have let in. The beginning of my vocation in youth ministry was over 20 years ago while I was still a youth myself. I often reflect that what I know now about faith, life and working with people would have made a huge difference to what I did in those early years. I was learning as I experienced and found myself ill-equipped to go deep into the practice of youth ministry.

At the ripe age of 21, I was given the responsibility of overseeing the youth program of a large congregation. I had received little training or mentoring, but drew on my intuition and deep commitment to building community for guidance. I worked hard to provide the youth in my programs with meaningful and challenging experiences, but as I didn't know how to go deep into a life of faith myself, trying to lead others there was daunting. Often I resorted to fun and games and left the "spiritual stuff" for the last ten minutes of youth group. I was so focused on the *how* of youth ministry that there wasn't much space to figure out *why* I was doing it at all.

I see now that I yearned for someone to help me figure out why God had called me to youth leadership and show me how I could translate my deep desires and best intentions into real actions. I needed someone to help me learn how to listen for the movement of Spirit and go deep into my own life in God.

Youth ministry is many things. It is the vibrant energy of a room full of teenagers. It is learning how to live in community and be a place for people to come wholly as they are and be accepted. It is fun, games, wacky adventures, laughter, and coming to know God. It is teaching and learning what it takes to be a person of faith. It is becoming more aware of how ordinary living is infused with the presence of God. It is coming to know how your life is connected with the life of Jesus and how the living Christ affects your life today.

Faith communities have a lot to offer youth in a postmodern world where generations seldom mix, where chaos and over-programming are rampant, where people don't have time and space to slow down. Even if they have trouble articulating or imagining it, most people are yearning for something that isn't yet part of their lives. Perhaps it's to be listened to, or understood. Perhaps it's having a place of shelter and community, a place to engage in experiences that focus attention on the Mystery of life and practices that draw us closer to God. Maybe it's a place to learn to pray. A place to turn to if our world is falling apart. A place to find loneliness quelled. A place to practice service. A place to be called brother or sister. A place to become someone new, to have life make more sense. A place to seek life in all its fullness. Your task as leader is to listen and discover what it is youth are seeking and then try and fill that need. It is what God has called us into community to do.

Imagine that it's your typical youth group night at the church. The youth have arrived and 15 of them are sitting around on couches in the youth room. There is chatter as you enter the room. Some of the youth notice you and say hello. They turn to you with expectant faces, ready to know what the plan is for the night. What are you going to do?

The activities you choose have everything to do with enabling the connectedness that all those hearts are yearning for, whether they articulate it or not. Your task is to think clearly about each activity you offer and ask the questions: Does this activity pull people toward God and enable understanding of themselves and their place in community? Does this activity work to create a sense of balance in the big picture of the youth ministry program?

Youth are often able to enter into conversations with a fully open nature. Are you matching their passion and willingness, or are you missing opportunities by making assumptions about what's boring and filling the space with fun and games? We underestimate the power and potential of youth. They are some of the most passionate people I know, hearts wide open to life and experience. Balance is required in youth ministry. Fun and games matched with opportunities to engage faith to greater depths. My hope is that this resource will give you the tools to do that.

This book will take you through practices that ask you to go deep into your own motivations, calling, and leadership. It will also provide you with simple practices of prayer to use with your own circle of youth. It contains

- *Reflections and questions about ways to think about your own faith, beliefs, and spiritual practices*
- *Practical tools and directions on how to set up spiritual practices for youth*
- *Practices of prayer, presence, and worship that can be incorporated into your youth ministry gatherings.*

One of my greatest lessons came through a youth's experience of God. I was at an annual weekend youth conference that had been full of youthful exuberance, amazing worship, fun, workshops, dancing, and community. At the end of the weekend, we had the classic wrap-up celebration of worship, singing and praising God together. Later, as I was standing at the door of the bus sending people off, a young man came up to me and gripped my hands, tears streaming down his face, his whole body shaking. I put my arms around him, thinking he needed comfort, and he said, "I don't know what just happened to me. I met God in there. I feel so warm, so alive. I'm not sure what to do. I can't understand what is happening to me."

He had experienced what I would call a dramatic movement of God's presence in his heart and life. He was overwhelmed and needed to share what he was feeling. His experience reminded me of the movement of the Spirit at Pentecost when God came in flame and wind. I have a feeling that young man has never forgotten that experience, as I have not forgotten it. Witnessing his experience took me to those places of new wine in my own faith. His experience opened an experience in me.

I encourage you to find ways to practice God in your own life. I encourage you to let go of fear; we learn by doing and then reflecting on the experience. I encourage you to go into the dark places where God comes in fire and trembling, and also into the light places of balloons, celebrations, and laughter. Learn to hold the hands of the youth you work with as they face challenge, learn, and grow. I encourage you to be who you really are in their midst. Don't be afraid to go deep into the love and mystery of God and the loving friendship in Christ. Don't be afraid to build a community of faith with joy and a sense of your own call. The Spirit is with you.

ICONS USED IN THIS BOOK

 The practice instructions take you through the steps involved in the practice and tell you what items you will need to have available. Practice icons alert you to the "hands on" stuff.

 Prayers can be said aloud or silently. Prayer icons make it easy for you to find a prayer if you are looking through the book for something to use.

 It's important to give clear instructions about the practices to youth. The "say-it-out-loud" icon indicates directions that leaders can use when explaining a practice to the group.

 This icon indicates a hand-out set of instructions.

 This icon indicates where music is used in practice. Specific pieces may be suggested or the choice may be left to the leader.

PART I

LeaDeR PRactICes

As a beginning youth minister, I longed for someone to help me learn how to go deep into my own life in God. I wonder if that has also been a yearning for you? Knowing yourself more deeply as a person of faith can be full of risk, challenge, comfort, joy and purpose. The fruits of your discoveries will benefit you and in turn all whom you encounter and minister to.

The experience of discovering God's expansive love and presence isn't just for youth: It can happen at any stage of life. The first step for you as a leader is to come to know yourself more deeply, incorporate that into your life and then learn to express your experience to others in a spirit of shared learning. Guiding youth in faith begins with practicing and strengthening your own faith. The goal is to enable yourself and youth to go deep into practicing God and living a life of faith.

Giving youth the gift of being able to speak authentically and articulately about faith is a great gift and perhaps it is a call in your life to be able to provide such openings. These next chapters will take you on an exploration of your own call, practice, and life of faith. Even if you feel like you've spent a lot of time trying to understand yourself in the context of your faith, I'd encourage you to go through the practices with your youth minister lens on.

If this is your first step on your path of going deep into your life in God, be welcome and know you do not go alone. Take seriously this work – it is the great work of your life.

CHAPTER 1

BEING CALLED TO LEADERSHIP

Leadership is a concept we often resist. It seems immodest, even self-aggrandizing, to think of ourselves as leaders. But if it is true that we are made for community, then leadership is everyone's vocation, and it can be an evasion to insist that it is not. When we live in the close-knit ecosystem called community, everyone follows and everyone leads. ~ Parker J. Palmer[1]

I remember well being part of a scene that has probably been lived out in numerous congregations over the years. It's a typical after-church coffee gathering. The youth leader has just walked in after an exhausting morning leading the youth Sunday school class. It was tough to get the youth to focus on the story and she doesn't feel good about how her program went. Her day began at 6 a.m. – the youth ministry job and going to school full-time is proving hard to manage and she didn't have time before this morning to look at the lesson plan. She grabs a cup of coffee as a member of the congregation corners her to reminisce about his own youth group experience 60 years ago. A youth group mom rounds the corner seeking volunteers for the thrift sale that's happening next week. Two youth come and ask what youth group will be about this week. They need to know, they need to make plans. The youth leader makes something up about doing something really fun. They say they will be there. Heading for the door, she hears the minister call from his office, "See you at the staff meeting on Wednesday; remember, you are bringing the muffins!" and as she passes the front desk, someone calls out, "We are so happy that we have you to work with our youth!"

She flees, wondering, *is this all there is?* Why does she feel so burdened? It seems that church has pretty much nothing to do with God or the mysterious Presence that she has known in other settings. It's like being part of a crazy workaholic family. She feels that no one acknowledges her own spiritual needs. She feels empty and pretty much alone.

Can I hear sighs echoing across the land? This youth leader's situation is a reflection of life in many institutions. Despite best intentions, church is generally focused on the *how* of ministry: committees, procedures, policies, stewardship drives, programs, and plans. Volunteers are lined up, the calendar is set, and we are off! Congregations and ministry staff can so easily find themselves caught in the trap of reacting to what seems most pressing, and focusing only on what, how, and who, with little reflection on *why* they are in ministry at all.

WHY?

The *how* of ministry is important, but how we do youth ministry must be balanced by reflecting on and engaging the question, *Why?*

In Proverbs we hear the words, "Where there is no vision, the people will perish." Living only in the *how* eventually leaves leader and participant craving deeper purpose and meaning. When we question *why*, we examine vision and purpose. If we simply follow tradition and routine, where is there space for God's movement to flow? Take a look back at that youth leader at that Sunday morning coffee hour. How is she being nourished?

 I suggest you enter into the questions below, either individually or as a congregation, to further explore the *why* behind your ministry with youth.

- *God is calling me, what am I hearing?*
- *Why do I care about engaging youth in the life of this congregation and providing a ministry for them?*
- *Why does the church want to offer youth what the world and culture cannot?*
- *Why are the gifts of a community of faith important to share?*
- *Why are my gifts as a youth leader important to share?*
- *How would I do youth ministry if I didn't have limits to my resources? Dream about where God is calling you to go.*

am I a YOUTH LeaDer?

God's call toward life in all its fullness can come strongly or softly, when you least expect it or when you know it for sure. It can come as sudden awareness or be something that has taken time to arise.

The word *vocation* comes from the Latin *vocare*, to call. Exploring your own call and what vocation means for you is a good place to start in your personal exploration of faith. God can call us from the inside out or from the outside in. Some people literally hear the voice of God nudging them toward a certain path or choice. You may have had a dramatic moment of awareness where suddenly all is clear, and you know what you have to do. Some people pay attention to the signs around them or what their inner voice is telling them. Or you may slide easily into a position based on the gifts you have been given.

God calls us through other people. Others may notice gifts in you and say something to you about them; they may ask you questions about ministry and how you see yourself participating in this kind of vocation. All these "callings" plant seeds within us and urge us to respond with a *Yes*.

Vocation does not come from willfulness. It comes from listening. I must listen to my life and try to understand what it is truly about – quite apart from what I would like it to be about – or my life will never represent anything real in the world, no matter how earnest my intentions. That insight is hidden in the word vocation itself, which is rooted in the Latin for 'voice.' Vocation does not mean a goal that I pursue. It means a calling that I hear. Before I can tell my life what I want to do with it, I must listen to my life telling me who I am.[2]

BEING CALLED

In some mysterious way, God is connected to our life and wants us to live it for the highest good. Our task is to listen for what our life could be; to know our gifts and how to use them to serve the world.

Being involved in youth leadership in a faith context is a deeply rewarding vocation that brings with it great gifts and huge challenges. Ministering to youth requires your full attention, concern, joy, and leadership commitment. It is an incredible gift simply to be called to consider it as a path.

One of the biggest privileges in working with youth is that they are opening up to many things for the first time. The world and its possibilities are there to be explored. And the discoveries they make have a lot to do with future paths taken. A youth leader can help inform those choices by providing opportunities for experiences of faith and community, where Spirit moves and life takes on new meaning and direction.

As someone called into youth ministry leadership, you will be the one who is responsible for intentionally teaching the practice of God. While the quality and nature of leadership is fundamentally important, what we really need to rely on and live out is God's active and sustaining presence. The greatest gift you can give youth is the awareness that the Creator wants to connect with them in a personal and real way. Knowing that a life of trust and faith will sustain them through the ups and downs of life is invaluable.

Does that sound daunting? Like a huge responsibility? Are you feeling like I'm asking you to be the wise, all-knowing youth leader and spiritual guide? If you are someone who has been called to work with youth in the context of a community of faith, there is no greater mission for your ministry than that. If that sounds like something that would be a real stretch for you, or it's something you've never done before, or the thought of it scares you, then the place to begin is with yourself. Spend some time focusing on what it is you believe, and what it is you can share about faith, and in discerning your own call to a life of service in ministry with youth.

It's up to you to develop the art of spiritual practice in your own life in order to be prepared to guide others into the practice of God. Ultimately, we practice to open to a deeper awareness of God's presence. When we practice God, life takes on new meaning and depth. There will be doubt, shaking and trembling, new possibilities, and abundant joy overflowing; all of which sustain us and provide a strong foundation from which to guide others.

In the rest of this chapter we'll explore some practices that will help you to connect with the leader within you. I offer some practices of journalling that I urge you to spend some time with. You may wish to create a leadership journal for yourself. Use it to engage the various practices in this book. If writing isn't for you, you may wish to speak aloud and explore these questions with someone else, or use a tape recorder. Leaving your responses within yourself may also be the way you engage. I do encourage you though to spend some significant time in the practice of understanding your own leadership and call.

I also encourage you to share your thoughts with another. When we share our stories they get deeper, richer, and more real. Opening up your story to another risks that you will be really seen. Life in all its fullness arises when we are truly seen and known in our challenges, struggles, joy, and call. And the stories become worth much more than if we keep them to ourselves because they can affect others.

CALLING ME, CALLING YOU

Through reflecting on the following questions you will be exploring your call to youth ministry. You may wish to spend some time alone reflecting on the questions first, and then discuss them with someone who can listen openly and help you go more deeply into your exploration of purpose and call (i.e., friend, colleague, spiritual director, or minister).

- *Have you had a specific experience of being called by God? Have you had a specific experience of being called to youth ministry? How would you describe those experiences to someone who really knows you?*
- *List the inner nudges, voices from others, thoughts, and dreams that have come to you regarding your ministry with youth or your potential for ministry. What are the experiences and conversations of your life saying to you about your call?*

LITANY OF CALL

The knock, the voice, the hand on the shoulder, the opening. The bush burning away, the miracle before your eyes. The knowing deep within. The surrender. The response.

God has been calling people from the beginning. Exploring call and understanding your purpose can help move you from simply creating programs and reacting in the moment to contemplating your primary purpose and what ministry means in your life.

Take some time to read through this litany of call stories from scripture and the modern world and reflect again on your sense of being called by God. Add other call stories you have connected with to this litany.

One day... Sitting in a boat on the Sea of Galilee, just passing the time and then suddenly I'm following him, a complete and total YES!

One Day... I'm tired of working in a job where I can't find meaning for myself. I keep coming back here every day, hating my work, starting to hate my life. Security, status, money all call me. It's the wrong call. Tomorrow I quit.

One Day... There I am, simply drawing water from the well. It's hot – midday – and he comes asking for a drink of water and the next thing I know I am sharing in Living Water and life feels different.

One Day... I'm walking through the refugee camp. I have never seen such emptiness in people's eyes, all human dignity stripped. But deep courage remains and I know I want to be around that kind of courage for a while.

One Day.... I'm walking through the desert and suddenly a burning bush appears and tells me to free the Hebrew people. Okay, how can I not go?

Today... Deep in my being I know what I am meant to do. I have a sense of my direction, my path, my reason for being in the world. I am aware of a door opening. Looking out, I see life differently.

Hey you... Ever thought of being a youth minister?

YOUR DEEPEST GIFTS

Mother Teresa said that passion is where the world's deepest needs and our deepest gifts connect. Mother Teresa knew all about that. It was how she lived. She was called to be a servant of the poor, seek justice in personal human transformation, pray, and know God. It's often easy to see where a person's passion lives. It is proclaimed in how they choose to use their lives, the activities they are engaged with, and what they speak about.

Our greatest gifts are given to us to be nurtured, brought to life, used, and shared. We are called to impact the people and the world around us in distinct and beautiful ways.

Sometimes youth have a hard time seeing their gifts. It takes time to understand the mysteries of what you have been given. Exploring the subject of gifts with youth and talking about the gifts you notice in them are great spiritual practices. But exploring and naming your *own* gifts is the first step.

The practice of naming gifts can be empowering and fulfilling.

Diversity makes a community strong. Each one leads in some way. Each gift is necessary to the creation and nurture of the community. Knowing what your gifts are not only influences the programs you provide, but helps you recognize areas of potential growth and where you can do the most giving.

 Spend some time reflecting on the gifts you have been given – your talents, passions, and skills. Make a list. You may ask two or three people who know you well to reflect on what they see as your deepest gifts. If you cannot see clearly into your life, create a list of all the things that give you joy and contentment. This list will give you hints about what your gifts may be.

Make your list now!

Once you've created the list, circle with a coloured marker the gifts that are most evident in your life and in your work with youth. Then go through the list again and notice which gifts are less present or obvious in your ministry. Circle those in a different coloured marker. Then spend some time journalling with these questions:

- *What feelings arise when you look over your gifts?*
- *What would engaging at a deeper level those gifts that are less present bring to your youth ministry?*

 Set three goals each for three of the gifts that are less present in your life. Write them down on a small card and keep them close by as a reminder.

Sample Goal

I seek to expand the gift of music leadership in my ministry with youth. My goal is to incorporate the gifts I have in music leadership more clearly into the programs I provide for youth. I will bring my guitar to the next youth group meeting and lead our closing song.

 Offer a prayer of thanksgiving for the gifts you have been given, or write one in your journal. If you are feeling at a loss, or tired and bored about your gifts, you may wish to ask God to reveal new ways that your gifts can be lived out. Pray deeply with gratitude for all the blessings that have come into your life because of the gifts you have been given.

Then ask yourself *where your greatest gifts connect with the world's great needs.*

The gifts that you gave me,
when you called me from the darkness
are the gifts that I give you.
I have nothing else to give.
And I offer what you offer,
when you breathed your love into me.
And your gifts so freely given,
take them now that I may live.

~ Jim Manley[3]

PERSONAL STATEMENT OF YOUTH MINISTRY

When God's love breathed your gifts into your life, amazing possibilities were created that will never be duplicated. Understanding your call and the gifts that you bring to the world is an important step in understanding yourself as leader. It can also be the beginning of deeper self-exploration.

 Take a pen and paper and write freely about what kind of leader you are in within the practice of ministry with youth. Write down "I am a leader" statements that incorporate your list of gifts from the previous practice and any other insights about your leadership that come to you. Take into account the ponderings that may have arisen from your work with the previous questions about call. This practice is about assessing what kind of leader you are, what gifts and skills you bring to leadership and how they can be lived out in your ministry. This practice is not necessarily about what kind of leader you hope to be. Work with what and who you are!

Examples

- *I am a leader who values community, connection, and sharing God's love.*
- *I am a leader who yearns for youth to feel that they have a place to run to – a refuge from the world.*
- *I am a leader who loves having fun, being silly, and sharing those times with youth.*
- *I am a leader who wants youth to know Jesus as a friend and have a personal relationship with him.*
- *I am a leader who wants to explore the gifts that other religions offer.*

Spend some time with this practice. Once you have completed your list of *I am a leader* sentences, read through them again, fine-tuning and re-writing until you have created a polished picture of your own practice of youth ministry. Share this personal statement with a mentor, colleague, or friend so that your statement gets out into the world. Share it with your co-leaders. Create one with the ministry team or youth committee you work with. Make one with youth themselves about their vision for their youth group.

Post your personal statement in your home or office where you can see it each day and be reminded of what you are trying to bring forth in your ministry. Be sure that each statement comes directly from who you are in the world of youth ministry, and speaks about your deep longings for wholeness and connection to that world.

It may be helpful to check in with your statement annually to rework it and re-energize your ministry through thoughtful reflection. Your gifts, passions, and areas of focus will change as time goes by. Pay attention to how you are evolving in your ministry.

DEALING WITH DOUBT AND FEAR

When you read over your explorations and personal statement, you may be confronted with a variety of feelings. You may feel empowered to get out there and live out your vision more fully. You may feel confident in your gifts. However, entering into new places in your leadership and following God's call in your life can bring uncertainty and doubt. God's call can take us to places that we are afraid to go.

 Look at a copy of your personal statement again and circle in one colour of pen the parts of the statement that bring you energy and joy, the places you know yourself to be well-equipped to take on a leadership role in youth ministry. Perhaps parts of the statement cause feelings of doubt or fear. Circle those parts in another colour. Notice how the page is starting to look. How many doubts do you have? How many joys? Are some of the joys and doubts the same? For each circled doubt and fear, explore in writing the specific way the fear or doubt is lived out.

Example

I am a leader who wants to share God's word by engaging with youth in Bible study.
Fear: I don't know enough about the stories in the Bible myself, and I get bored easily. How can I make them come alive for youth?

Notice the doubts and fears that are there on paper. Pray through the list, asking for strength and courage to face and move through the fear and doubt into service.

There are actions you can take to lessen or overcome each of your doubts and fears. Work through your list again and write ways to work with them so that you can move from fear to confidence. Remember to be realistic.

Example

I am a leader who wants to share God's word by engaging with youth in Bible study.

Fear: I don't know enough about the stories in the Bible myself and I get bored easily. How can I make it come alive?

Action: I will attend a Bible study at church once a week and become a leader who studies the scriptures so that I will be more able to engage myself and lead others enthusiastically.

You may wish to symbolically "cast off" your fears and doubts once you have finished working through them. You might burn them in a fire, place them under a rock in a park, rip the paper into tiny pieces and keep them in a special box. Whatever you do, know that God's light and presence in your life can assist you in transcending all your fears.

a LIFE OF SERVICE

Serving is different from helping. Helping is based on inequality... When you help you use your own strength to help those of lesser strength. If I'm attentive to what's going on inside of me when I'm helping, I find that I'm always helping someone who's not as strong as I am, who is needier than I am. People feel this inequality. When we help we may inadvertently take away from people more than we could ever give them; we may diminish their self-esteem, their sense of worth, integrity and wholeness. When I help I am very aware of my own strength. But we don't serve with our strength, we serve with ourselves. We draw from all of our experiences. Our limitations serve, our wounds serve, even our darkness can serve. The wholeness in us serves the wholeness in others and the wholeness in life. The wholeness in you is the same as the wholeness in me. Service is a relationship between equals.

~ Rachel Naomi Remen

We have looked at call in our lives, what our gifts are, and how we can activate them. We've acknowledged the fears and doubts that come with being called into new possibilities. The next place to explore is the heart of our life of service.

Practicing youth ministry is a call to a life of service. It's not the easiest way to live. You won't make a fortune, the hours are long and unpredictable, people may disappoint you, and sometimes you will feel like you are swimming against the stream.

Ministry with youth casts us into the thick of the real world. Youth leaders are called to respond to real people and their needs: people who spill and cry, freak out or laugh hysterically; people who need things for their physical and spiritual comfort, survival, and growth; people who make mistakes, or who stun you with their brilliance and presence; people who seek, doubt, question, and proclaim their truth. So many complex needs and so many roles to fill. I cherish this simple response: *an open heart, loving God; open hands, loving people.*

There are many stories of people who have chosen the call and vocation of service over financial gain, status, and personal reward. I'd like to share with you the story of Hanley Denning, a teacher from the United States who visited Guatemala in the 1990s. During her travels, she visited the Guatemala City garbage dump, one of the largest in Central America, where people scrape survival out of burning piles of rubbish. Hanley saw very young children picking garbage with their parents and it called her to act. She sold all her possessions, moved to Guatemala, and began a project called *Safe Passage*, an after-school program for hundreds of children. She created a safe and caring refuge for countless children who no longer have to work picking garbage in the dump. Hanley died tragically in an automobile accident in Guatemala City in 2007 but her life of service continues in the children and volunteers of *Safe Passage*.

My godfather, Edward, was a layperson in the United Church of Canada who was active in the same congregation for 78 years. He lived a life deeply rooted in service, giving tirelessly to the ministry of his congregation and to many charities and causes. He felt a strong call to ministry throughout his life, and lived it out through his commitment to helping people. He served on church committees, took people grocery shopping, and when he couldn't get out anymore himself, he used the telephone as his ministry tool, talking to many people over the course of the day. His service legacy continued even after his death with the financial gifts he left to many organizations and individuals.

Your life of service in youth ministry may take on meaning and depth that you cannot now imagine. If you choose a life of service, your own life will be served in deep ways; the seeds that you plant in others are planted in you as well.

 Bring to mind someone whose life of service has had an impact on your life. It could be someone close to you, someone that you have a connection with, someone in history, or someone you know of but haven't met.

Spend some time journalling or in conversation, reflecting on the following questions.

- *What are the gifts this person brings to your life?*
- *Can you embrace the image of a life of service for yourself?*
- *Can you embrace the image of a life of service in youth ministry for yourself?*
- *What gives you the most passion about contributing to the world in this way?*
- *What might you be called to give up so that this way of life can be lived out?*

Write a letter of thanks to the person you named above. If you can, send it to that person. If that isn't possible, read it to someone else, telling them about this special person in your life. It is rare for people to fully understand their impact in the lives of others; let's take every opportunity possible to share how we have been blessed by the lives of others.

PRAYER OF COMMITMENT

 Share this prayer with yourself, another person, or your congregation if you feel ready to commit yourself to serving other people. You may also write your own prayer of commitment.

Light a candle. Say this prayer aloud or to yourself.

 Oh God of service, of giving and receiving,
I am your servant. I stand with open hands ready to serve and ready to receive.
I bring my whole self, my light and my dark, my over-functioning, my missing wisdom, my seeking of balance, my great gifts, and my faith.
Oh God who serves me, I give thanks for this call to a life of meaning and passion.
For the struggle that will come, I ask for help.
For the joy that will come, I give thanks.
I commit myself to a life of service for your people and for your world. Help me in all the ways I will need help. Help me to be humble in my service and aware of your presence with me always. Amen.

SO YOU FINALLY GET TO LOOK AT WHAT!

This is an opportunity for you to further develop your youth ministry, gifts and vision statement. This is where you get to be practical, hands on, and task oriented!

 Take a look at your vision statement (personal statement) again and brainstorm about ways you may effectively engage each sentence in ministry with youth. Write the first thoughts that come into your awareness. When you've gone through each sentence once, read them through again and brainstorm a second idea for each one.

Examples

I am a leader who values community, connection, and sharing God's message of love.

> *Have a welcome ritual for new people attending youth group; integrate a check-in into the beginning of each meeting; have youth leave each meeting hearing or seeing the words* God loves you *in some form.*

I am a leader of Youth who loves to have fun, be silly, and share those times with youth.

> *Create space for laughter and games at each youth meeting. As a leader, don't sit on the sidelines; play hard as they play hard.*

You get the idea? Go to it with your own statement. When you are finished, share it with someone. Integrate your ideas into your ministry. Use them when you are stuck for an idea, when you need to remember why you are there, when too many people ask you about numbers and "the plan." Remember your purpose and your passion and let that guide your ministry. Your responses to the *why* question in your life will inspire the work of *what*.

WRAPPING UP

You will now have talked through or written in your journal a reflection on your call to ministry a list of the gifts that God has given you to use in your service in the world, your own personal statement on the practice of youth ministry, a look at the fears and areas of energy that arise from your statement, a reflection on your own life of service, and a reflection on hands-on practices related to your personal youth ministry statement.

Conversation about leadership and your personal gifts will come up again and again as your life shifts and you practice being a reflective leader. Our faith doesn't stand still and neither does God's presence. It moves and changes as you move and change. The key is to be open and listen for what God may be urging you toward. Be open to walking through doors you never imagined.

BLESSING

The light that graced your face on the day of your arrival blesses you each day.
The Holy Presence that moved on the waters of creation moves in your life each day.
The Creator, who knows all knowing, seeks to know you each day.
God of your life calls you to go deep into your own life and live with passion and purpose each day.
Serve with open heart and open hands, love people and love God each day.
Amen.

---

1   Palmer, Parker J. *Let Your Life Speak Listening for the Voice of Vocation* (San Francisco: Jossey-Bass, 2000) Page 4
2   Ibid.
3   "The Gifts That You Gave Me" – Words and music © 1976 by James K. Manley

CHAPTER 2

DEEPENING LEADERSHIP

You, sent out beyond your recall,
Go to the limits of your longing.
Embody me.
Flare up like flame
And make big shadows you can move in.
Let everything happen to you: beauty and terror.
Just keep going. No feeling is final.
Don't let yourself lose me.
Nearby is the country they call life.
You will know it by its seriousness.
Give me your hand.

~ Rainer Maria Rilke[1]

This chapter is about setting the intention to let the awareness of God enter more deeply into your own life, and then exploring practices to enable that. If you are called to youth leadership, understanding and exploring your beliefs and how you relate to the Biblical story, and having your own practice of connection with the Divine are ways to make your leadership more effective. It's pretty much mandatory to have spiritual practice in your own life if you plan to lead youth into spiritual practice.

Intention is setting an outcome or goal, and then *yearning* for it to come to fruition. Intention begins creation. It is a decision; a practice of commitment and trust that can begin and end each day for you. Intention involves trusting the inner workings of your life and God. Intention involves your heart. Each person's intention will be different. But whatever it is, however you do it, just begin to practice intention today!

 Holy One, I choose life. I choose openness. I choose beauty, and faith. I choose to create. In all the things I intend for my life and the life of the world, oh God hear my prayer, and in your love and understanding, answer.
Amen.

The paths to God are as diverse as the many people on earth, and your practice will be unique to you. You may be holding to practices that you did as a child. Your practice may feel like a good and safe place to be, full of gratitude and joy. It may also be full of doubt and uncertainty. You may be struggling with your practice and seeking new ways to engage your faith. You may not have any practice at all. Just remember that each life is a unique pilgrimage. Try to cease judging where you have been.

It's time to start just where you are. The beauty of spiritual practice is that it's never too late to start something new. You may wish to experiment with some of the practices outlined in this resource. See which ones call you. Try out some that seem challenging. The practices that seem most unlike us or most difficult are the ones to pay attention to.

A fellow youth worker recently reflected to me that he could never sit still, and had real trouble understanding what silence and still contemplative prayer were all about. He shared with me how he challenged himself to attend a *Lectio Divina*[2] group at his congregation, even though he thought it was the last thing that would work for him. When he walked into the room and found four people sitting around a candle, he nearly bolted. But something convinced him to stay and give it a try. The people in the group gently taught him the practice. They encouraged him and offered support when the sitting and stillness became difficult. He sat through that first session not totally convinced that he could ever do it again, but something called him to go back, again and again. He then integrated *Lectio Divina* into his personal spiritual practice. It was a practice that he, as an active extroverted youth minister, never could have imagined himself doing.

Often what we most need is beyond our ability to see. I encourage you to challenge yourself and expand your practice in some way. Go into the places that feel uncomfortable for you, for in those places gifts are waiting.

Given all the focus on the *how* of ministry, it is easy to let a personal practice slip away. We can bring tremendous depth to our ministry with youth when we have lived through our own questions and doubts. We must know ourselves and how the Divine is lived out in our lives before we can teach others what that means. Connection with the Divine will be the thing that sustains us in the end. The right practices for you will come into your life. Your task is to respond and experience with an open heart, trusting that you are receiving all that you need.

The scriptures mean different things to different people. Understanding and exploring your beliefs and how you relate to the Biblical story and to Jesus will help ground you in the fundamentals of Christian leadership. For some, scripture is the literal cornerstone on which all else is built; for others, it offers a way into meaning, like myth. The stories help some know how to live; for others, they are a source of frustration and challenge. The stories of our faith are meant to "bring out" something in everyone, something that will lead us to choose fullness of life.

It is a common refrain in youth ministry that it is difficult to get youth to relate to the Bible stories. How, in an age of mp3, gaming, and Facebook, can a simple story about some people in a boat on the Sea of Galilee be interesting? As youth leaders, we must feel comfortable with the stories, and be willing and able to interpret them in ways that connect with today's youth. If we can find our own place in the ancient stories, then we can demonstrate that stories of faith are still being written today. The writers of ancient scripture can inspire and move us in the same way that modern-day poets, writers, musicians, and film-makers do. I urge you to discover more about what the stories of the Christian faith mean for you.

If you are truly engaged in your ministry, it can be a tough gig. You will be called to fill many roles in your work with youth, parents, church leaders, committees, congregations, and co-workers. The experience of youth leadership has led to many youth leaders burning out. It is not uncommon for a youth leader to start in a position super-keen, working more than their hours, caught up in their commitment and passion for the ministry, and then be unable to sustain the pace. Their own faith gets lost in the business of life. They feel unsupported and in the end leave, feeling lost and like a failure.

Burnout is something that leaders should acknowledge and seek ways to avoid. It is not God's call to work to a stage of burnout and it is not the church's call to allow that. Seek out and maintain practices of balance. Supportive and connected friends and mentors will also help you maintain a balanced way of life.

WHaT DO I BeLIeVe?

 Spend some time reflecting on the following questions and statements, perhaps making notes.

    Doing this inner faith and belief work requires courage and trust. It can stir things up and bring questions and insights to the surface. It's important to process the feelings you have. You may want to share your thoughts with someone.

- *What are the biggest questions I have about God, faith, and myself right now?*
- *If someone looked at my life, how would they know that I am a person of faith?*

Write down thoughts, questions, images, and words about what you believe about the following. Spend thoughtful time on all of the themes, coming to a place where you can articulate your responses clearly. Savour the questions you have, knowing that seeking responses will bring you more deeply into your life. Spend time talking with others about your common and differing beliefs. Celebrate and notice all the ways people come to faith.

- *God*
- *Jesus*
- *The Holy Spirit*
- *Christ*
- *Salvation*
- *Sin*
- *Resurrection*
- *The Bible*

- *Church*
- *Other religions*
- *Prayer and conversation with God*
- *What happens when we die*
- *The purpose of life*
- *The presence of God in my life*

JESUS IN MY LIFE

From the life of Jesus arose the Christian faith.

For some, Jesus is the living God. For others, Jesus is saviour of the world, prophet, messenger, storyteller, or God in human form. Wherever you stand on the question of Jesus, it is important to be able to clearly articulate how his life is connected with your own; to spend time prayerfully understanding not only the historical Jesus, but also the living Christ. If you are a leader of youth in a Christian context, not talking about Jesus is not an option. Figure out how he fits into your own life.

 Find a picture of Jesus that draws you. You may search online or use an art book. Choose a picture that you are comfortable spending some time with and then read through the following meditation. Gaze at the image you have chosen. You may wish to write down words or insights that come to you while you are studying the image.

© istockphoto.com

One life.
Jesus lived on this earth.
He was born, lived and breathed, rejoiced and celebrated, had a ministry, questioned, suffered, was judged and killed. He shared stories and practiced miracles. He was many different things. He asked his followers, "Who do you say that I am?" Over 2,000 years later, he still asks, "Who do you say that I am?"

Some questions to reflect on:

- *How is my life connected to the life of Jesus? How is this evident?*
- *What message of Jesus do you most want to live out and share?*
- *What does being a disciple of Jesus mean to you?*
- *How is yours a life that follows Jesus?*

FINDING YOUR STORY

Lectio Divina is an ancient method of reading and savouring sacred texts in order to gain understanding of how they relate to your own life.[2]

 Choose one of the call stories below to work with. Look up the passage and find a quiet space to work. Light a candle to help centre you into this time of holy reading and listening. If you are doing this practice with someone else, take turns reading the passage.

After the first reading, sit in silence for a few minutes, and then share aloud or write one word that stood out for you in the passage.

After the second reading, sit in silence for a few minutes, and then share aloud or write a question that comes to mind.

After the third reading, sit in silence for a few minutes and reflect on how this passage relates to and connects with your own life and call. Share or journal your response.

The Call of Abram (Abraham) and Sarai (Sarah) – *Genesis 12:1–9*
Esther's Call – *Esther 4:13–17*
The Call of Samuel – *I Samuel 3:1–10*
The Call of the Disciples – *Matthew 4:18–22*
The Call of Paul – *Acts 9:3–19*

Offer a prayer of thanks for the gifts of this practice.

THE BIBLE

Hold a Bible in your hands. Look at it; notice the binding, the cover. Feel the weight of it. Flip through it, noticing the table of contents, familiar names, stopping occasionally to read a line. If the Bible were included on bestseller lists, it would be a rare week when it didn't hit number one.

Hold the book in your hands and consider its impact on your life.

- *What is your relationship with the scriptures of the Christian faith?*
- *How do you use them in your life (daily, weekly, monthly, never)?*
- *What word, line, or story from scripture has spoken to you recently?*
- *What stories relate to your ministry with youth?*
- *What are your key questions and concerns about the ancient texts?*
- *What modern sources of inspiration (poems, songs, articles, essays) have spoken to you? How do you use them? How else could you imagine using them?*

HOW DO I PRACTICE?

The following questions encourage you to explore how you connect with the Divine.

Spend some time journalling or in conversation.
- *How do you practice God in your own life?*
  Make a list of all the intentional ways you engage in spiritual practice.
- *What practices would you like to try?*
  You might like to read through the practices in this resource.

- *What practices seem most difficult for you?*
- *What practices could you let go of so that new energy and passion can come into your life?*
- *How do you describe your engagement with spiritual practice?*

AN APPOINTMENT WITH GOD

 Look at your calendar for the coming week and book an appointment with God. Schedule in **at least** one session of personal spiritual practice during the week. If this is a completely new experience, consider starting with one 15-minute session and working your way up to longer and more frequent sessions in the weeks to come.

Choose a time of day that works best for you – perhaps first thing in the morning, or last thing before bed, or afternoon tea with God. Choose a time that you can commit to. It's up to you to set the time frame you need to encounter God. Be intentional.

Set the space. Make it comfortable, light a candle, have a journal and/ or Bible nearby. Choose a practice to engage. Sing if a song comes to you; pray out loud if a prayer comes; sit in silence if that is how you are called to be. Focus on intentionally immersing yourself in the way of God for the time you have given yourself. You may want to start by grounding yourself by breathing in and out a few times and saying with your breath:

I am here. God is here.

Commit to some weeks of this practice. At the end of that time, notice what is different about you. Journal about what you notice.

MENTORS AND FRIENDS

We are pilgrims on a journey.
Fellow travellers on the road.
We are here to help each other
Walk the mile and bear the load.

~ Richard Gillard[3]

In their book *The Godbearing Life*, Ron Foster and Kenda Creasy Dean reflect that people require a number of different kinds of relationships in order to thrive in life and ministry. They suggest that we all need circles of friendship in order to be fully human. It is the circle that includes our soul friends, or the people who pull us toward God, that I am most interested in understanding.

A soul friend is someone who reminds you about God's presence in your life. It is important to have at least one *anam cara* (Gaelic for soul friend) who knows your life and work intimately and to whom you can go to seek counsel and pray with; someone who can listen and hear you. Your soul friend may simply help you remember your own place as a person of faith in this crazy world and encourage you to continue practicing. An intentional soul friend relationship dwells in the realm of God and can be one of life's deepest blessings.

Examining how you receive and give the gift of soul accompaniment is a component in growing your ministry to a place of health, strength, and impact.

 Spend some time reflecting on the support you have in your life. Draw a small circle that represents you in the middle of a piece of paper. Then draw small circles at various representative distances for the people who support you. Connect them to you with lines. Are the lines strong and bold, or are they weak and barely there? How close are the other circles to you?

Once you have finished the drawing, answer the following questions.

- *Who are the soul friends who intentionally pull you toward God?*
- *What are the qualities of your connection with them?*
- *If you don't think you have a soul friend, what impact do you imagine having one might have on your life?*
- *Is there someone you could imagine developing a soul friendship with? What steps could you take to begin to foster such a connection?*
- *Are you a soul friend to anyone? What do you value about that relationship?*

If you want to bring soul friendship into your life, pray about it and set the intention. Also be intentional about thanking the people who offer you support.

WHAT OTHER WORLDS DO YOU SING IN?

Youth ministry is demanding and can easily use up all your resources and time if you aren't careful in your response to need. All ministry leaders need places where other gifts, talents, interests, and relationships can develop. Whether it is hiking, stamp collecting, or turning a pot on a wheel, activities outside of ministry work are an important part of your own practice and deeply sustaining to your faith. Connecting with the world "out there" also offers an opportunity to hear from those outside our usual ministry orbit. Savour what they have to tell you. They may be the way God is speaking to you.

Reflect and journal on these questions.

- *Which practices, interests, and people outside my youth ministry work nurture me?*
- *When and how do I make the time to nurture those connections and relationships?*
- *What practices and interests have I lost touch with? Do I long for them? Do I feel called to re-activate them in my life?*

Then look at your calendar for the next month and set aside some time to engage an interest outside the church. Perhaps reclaim something that you miss doing. Maybe it's going to the beach, riding a horse, playing sports with friends, or baking bread. You get the idea. Make a plan and do it. There are many other worlds out there for you to explore and be enlivened by. Remember them!

Once you have spent the time, take yourself out for coffee and reflect and journal on how you felt about engaging that interest. What gift or challenge did it bring into your life? Look at your calendar again and set your next *my other world* date.

SABBATH – DELIGHTING IN THE WAY OF NOT DOING

The concept of keeping one day holy and for God goes way back. Here's what Jesus said about it.

Are you tired? Worn out? Burned out on religion? Come to me. Get away with me and you'll recover your life. I'll show you how to take a real rest. Walk with me and work with me – watch how I do it. Learn the unforced rhythms of grace. I won't lay anything heavy or ill-fitting on you. Keep company with me and you'll learn to live freely and lightly.[4]

So much of how we live in the modern world moves us toward activity and busy-ness and away from not doing and the renewal that comes from rest. Our days are filled with tasks and seem too short. Having to constantly respond to "so much" brings stress. Finding time to practice rest and Sabbath often takes more strength than we have, although deep down we yearn for it. An incongruent process can emerge when we teach reflection and prayer but don't find time to practice ourselves. We read about keeping Sabbath but we fall short of developing a sustaining practice of Sabbath in our own lives. The quick one-minute prayer as you drift off to sleep after a day of obligations and errands doesn't really count.

Sabbath involves being still, listening for God, and renewing mind and body. Sabbath time urges us to slow down and wake up to what is happening in our inner and outer lives.

How do we find the time to practice Sabbath in our own lives? How do we find a way to cease doing and hold one day holy?

 Spend some time journalling the following questions and reflecting. Remember *intention*. You have to choose that Sabbath will happen and make it a priority in your life. Learn from others, and keep company with those who know how to chill out!

- *How is the Sabbath lived out in your life right now?*
- *What could you imagine opening space for in your life if you really practiced Sabbath?*
- *What do you need to stop doing in order to make space for a day of rest?*
- *How would it be possible to slow down for one day a week?*
- *How do you imagine your day of rest? Write down what you will do and set a date.*

Retreat

In a ministry of giving and service, it is important to take a break longer than a one-day Sabbath periodically. A retreat is different from a vacation. It means going away to a quiet place and entering into a time of resting and listening to Spirit. It means taking seriously the Sabbath themes in your life and practicing them.

The kind of retreat I am talking about here involves minimal program (perhaps worship to begin and end each day), some conversation with a spiritual director or a soul friend, and plenty of time for doing what your heart, mind, and body feel called to do. Many retreat centres offer group retreats where you will be with other people in a time of retreat from the world and directed by a facilitator or spiritual director. Perhaps you have access to a cabin or house away from your context where you could go on your own retreat. It may be advisable to begin your exploration of personal retreat in a setting with some structure, in a place with little distraction.

The rules for personal retreat are quite simple. Come as you are. Bring all your joy, stress, and frustration, whatever you've got. Bring with you only the things that pull you toward God. Take no work. Take off your watch, eat food that is pleasing to you when you are hungry, sleep when you need to sleep, breathe deeply, pay attention to your dreams, get out into nature. Cease checking your e-mail and using your cell phone. Notice the details. Pray. Seek stillness. Listen for God.

If going away for a number of days is not possible given the context of your life, try setting up a half or full day retreat, where you put on hold the things of "ministry" and focus on prayer, stillness, things that bring you pleasure, and Holy Presence. If you have never done a personal retreat before, I would encourage you to try.

Recently I took an extroverted friend on his first personal retreat. Something had compelled him to come with me, even though he never would have imagined he could do such a thing. During the first few hours at the retreat house he kept asking me, "What do I do?" He needed to fill the space. The concepts of stillness and responding to his life with rest were so foreign to him that it took him some time to adjust.

In the end he didn't want to leave. He had encountered the world of silence and peace for the first time, and newness and vibrancy came to him, along with deep rest and the reflection on his own life that he was in deep need of.

 A sample day of retreat
- *Be in the present moment*
- *Let yourself wake up naturally*
- *Pray on rising*
- *Eat breakfast mindfully*
- *Walk in nature*
- *Notice*
- *Sing to yourself, sing to God*
- *Nourish your body with wholesome food*
- *Journal, practice* Lectio Divina, *pray, practice walking prayer/ mindful walking, walk a labyrinth*
- *Close the day in an intentional way*
- *Sleep when you are tired*
- *Pray before sleep*
- *Pay attention to your dreams*

---

1 "Gott spricht zu jedem…/God speaks to each of us…", from *Rilke's Book of Hours: Love Poems to God* by Rainer Maria Rilke, translated by Anita Barrows and Joanna Macy, copyright © 1996 by Anita Barrows and Joanna Macy. Used by permission of Riverhead Books, an imprint of Penguin Group (USA) Inc.

2 For more on *Lectio Divina*, see chapter 5.

3 "The Servant Song" by Richard Giller, copyright 1977 *Scripture in Song*/Maranatha Music/ASCAP (All rights administered by Music Services.) All rights reserved. Used by permission.

4 Matthew 11:28–30, *The Message*

CHAPTER 3

PRACTICING GOD WITH YOUTH

Everything on earth has its own time
and its own season.

~ Ecclesiastes

Life in our modern world calls us to spend most of our time focused on the details of living. The goal of practicing God is to take us from living on the surface to touching the inner world below. The often intangible presence of God is in this soft place. It's the place where we question, *How is my spirit today? How do I see God? What am I yearning for?*

Each life yearns for connection and wholeness. However, we cannot judge people by the degree to which they seek these things; there is no "right" way to God. Ideally, youth leaders nudge people onto their own path of yearning and faith by teaching them how to encounter, engage, and manifest their connection with the Holy One.

In my work with young people, I have witnessed them giving themselves over fully to the experience they are engaged in. Their exuberance, reverence, concentration, and delight in being fully present to themselves and to the practice of God is stunning. All they need is a guide. Your task as a leader is to provide the opportunity, then step back and allow them to walk their own path. To witness the awakening and growth of Spirit in a life is one of deepest joys of being in youth ministry.

Practicing God with youth requires preparation on behalf of the leader. Paying attention to some key components will help keep practices open, safe, and honest.

- **Be Open**

  Engage the practices enthusiastically, try new things, and participate fully, trusting that God will lead you.

- **Meet youth where they are**

  Use and create practices that engage the seeker, the one who needs to belong, the questioner, the one who needs to move, the one who is lost. Provide a variety and balance of experiences.

- **Practice**

  Remember that to practice means doing something over and over. Find places to introduce practices into your ministry on regular basis. Encourage people to return to the same practices and try new ones. Remember to practice yourself.

- **Be intentional**

  Clearly lay out your intentions for yourself, the youth, and your youth ministry program with respect to spiritual practices. For example, your intentions may be to

- enrich the spiritual lives of youth;
- enable youth to encounter Christ through a variety of practices;
- connect with the Divine Mystery.

- **Pay attention**

  Engage the body, mind, and heart. Pay attention to the specific needs of youth you are working with. Be sensitive to adapting the plan and working in the moment to deepen the practice.

- **Gather resources**

  Use both ancient and modern sources of inspiration. Create your own practices, use the practices in this resource, talk with spiritual leaders, learn about and engage the world at a deeper level until the right practices for you and your group are encountered.

- **Create space**

  Pay close attention to how the practice space is set up. Create a beautiful place in which to practice. Use space in the natural world, or transform an ordinary indoor space.

- **Clear direction**

  Give clear direction, in spoken and written form, on how to do the practices, then step back and allow people to practice in their own way and time. There is no right or wrong way to practice.

- **Breathe deeply**

  Remain flexible and spontaneous. Watch for opportunities to practice together in all aspects of life. Live in the moment.

- **Embrace ritual**

  Repeat practices and create rituals specific to who you are as a group.

Youth leaders need to take the time to listen and share with youth. Often I've heard youth and young adults express a sense of feeling lost, of having little to support them as they go through big issues in their lives. What they yearn for in those moments is tangible connection, a place to belong, and to be listened to.

Spiritual practices provide intentional times for individuals to work either alone or with others. They create soft places where we allow ourselves to open to God's presence and become more vulnerable and aware of feelings and emotions that may have been ignored. Youth leaders need to ensure that youth feel safe being with and expressing their feelings, and that they are not left alone with those feelings.

Intentional spiritual practice is foreign to current modern youth culture. Sometimes it is not present in the youth ministry program either. Wouldn't it be amazing if youth could walk into the youth group meeting knowing that they are fully accepted for who they are, and that the space they enter is a safe place to ask questions and receive the gifts of God? Ideally, youth group offers a way of life that youth may not have imagined for themselves. A way of life full of the love of the Creator.

During my research, I talked with youth who experienced some of the intentional spiritual practices outlined in this resource. I asked them to share what the practices meant to them.

I always liked the spiritual practices. It is the time in my life where I can let go of everything, and become everything I want to be. Then, once it is all through, I can put all my energy into becoming that person.

Nathaniel, age 18

I find that sometimes I get so busy that I don't have time to think about the things in my life and their effects on my well-being. Relationships, jobs, habits... have such an impact on the way we feel and the way we function – through spiritual practices I noticed that I come to accept a lot of things in my life that I would have otherwise... blocked out. The solitude and set time to reflect and rediscover what is in your heart is irreplaceable and priceless.

Molly, age 16

I find God in the spiritual practices time. I understand how God can exist. I just go inside myself and find peace and find Jesus around me.

Derek, age 16

My favourite part of spiritual practices has always been the silence. It doesn't matter if I'm writing a letter to God or playing with clay. That one hour of silence is kind of like the quiet time our parents put us through when we were younger, now lost in our noisy lives. Somehow, that one restriction opens up every sense, bringing an amazing spiritual connection.

Dora, age 16

I was peaceful. I felt peaceful and I began to like myself a little more.

Jen, age 15

Leaders need to practice alongside youth. It's not okay for you to set up a practice space and then stand on the sidelines and watch. The practices need to speak to you as well as to the youth. You will all gain from the practices.

It's important to engage all of the senses by having practices where people can move and use their bodies in creative responses – touching, tasting, seeing, smelling, hearing, and feeling God's presence. Many of the practices in this resource encourage open-heartedness. It is in the realm of the heart that we connect with God. Our open hearts allow us to feel the movement of Spirit.

It's also important to watch for occasions to practice during everyday activities. Perhaps on a hike with your group you notice that people are quietly walking on the path and seem open to practice. Invite them to go off on their own for ten minutes to pray. When they come back, have them share how this felt.

It is easy to focus on what is to come and lose track of being in the moment. You may be thinking about how the heck you are going to make a fire and cook dinner since all the wood appears wet. You may be thinking about the program for next week and miss the opportunity to stop in the woods and smell life all around. Being present in the moment is an opportunity to let go of expectation. Letting go of how you think something should be will be helpful in engaging practices in a spontane-ous and responsive way. Trust that God is part of your experience. There ultimately may not be a tomorrow. There is just this moment, and as we live into this way to be in God, we live into the possibility that every part of life is spiritual practice.

Making a Space Sacred

A space set up with the intention of enhancing an experience of the sacred can be called a sacred space. A sacred space allows people to feel reverent, still, safe, at peace, celebratory, excited, close to God, and loving. It allows questioning and wonder. People feel comfortable about bringing their whole selves there. A sacred space encourages us to stop, wake up, and centre our hearts in God.

A sacred space can be anywhere. It can be a space that you have set up indoors, or it could be a spot in the natural world that God has already arranged.

Creating sacred space involves paying attention to how the senses will be stimulated in that space. Where are the eyes drawn? What will the ears hear? What might the nose smell in the air? What comforts will the body feel? Will there be a time to taste life?

It may feel strange at first to engage your whole body in worship and spiritual practice. It's like a reawakening – a remembering that God created us whole beings with parts made to dance, kneel, smell, and embrace. Imagine yourself as a child jumping to the music, walking to the front of the sanctuary open and willing to take in whatever comes. Wouldn't it be glorious to be that child again? Who made the rule that we cannot bring all of ourselves into a worship space? Certainly not God. Somehow we seem to forget about all our wonderfully and fearfully made parts when we simply go in, sit down, and receive.

I'd like to tell you about Daniel, a highly intelligent and courageous 14-year-old young man who happened to be blind. He taught me that sight is only one way for us to "see" God and one another. He was always in my mind as I created programs. His presence allowed us all to think beyond the context of seeing with our eyes. He was a gift to my ministry – I gained the understanding that there is more than one way to engage the world, more than one way to see, and more than one sense to employ.

Think of the ways worship spaces stimulate our senses: banners, candles, lights, stained glass, prayer wheels, sacred texts, statues of saints and prophets, altars, burning incense, art, menorahs, icons and crosses. Sensory experiences require a different kind of attention beyond the physical response. They ask for the attention of an open heart. They ask us to put the world "out there" on hold and enter into a space set apart, a time of Sabbath, a time to really notice.

Remember that sacredness can be found in the darkest places too, during the hardest times of life. A hospital room, the poorest street, a time of disaster are all places that hold the sacred. The sacred universe is available to us at all times and is everywhere.

How a space is set up is important, but more important is how we are in that space. Your presence as a leader in a sacred space can draw people into understanding how they are called to be open to God. Your presence can set the intention for your whole group. By noticing and practicing mindfulness and openness in the moment of connection with a sacred space, you call others to be open as well.

Again, we return to intention. How do we enter a space? How do we notice? How do we ask questions? How do we sit together? How do we form community? Your actions as a leader will be the key to allowing everyone around you to feel the place you are in as sacred. Perhaps the connections between people are the most sacred spaces of all.

ENGAGING THE SENSES IN YOUR SPACE

 Imagine your own typical youth meeting and do an assessment on the use of the senses in response to the questions below.

This is a good practice to do with another youth leader. You could do an assessment of your meeting spaces, walking through them, paying attention to how youth see them. Set goals together to help make your meeting spaces fabulous, warm, vibrant places for youth to be.

- *What does the space you are meeting in look like?*
- *How are people welcomed into the space?*
- *What senses are engaged during the course of the gathering?*
- *What senses are not engaged?*
- *How could you bring about more connection with the senses?*
- *How could you bring about more connection with the Holy?*
- *What will you do to engage the senses and set up the space with sacredness in mind?*

Set a goal to do one specific thing in the next month to set sacred space in your youth ministry program.

SETTING UP A SPIRITUAL PRACTICES EXPERIENCE

There are many ways to incorporate intentional spiritual practice into a youth ministry program. This resource contains practices that can be used individually or as part of a collection. You may choose one practice for each youth group gathering and explore it as a group. You may choose to bring a number of the practices together and set up a room with "practice stations." Have gentle music playing to create a mood of contemplation and invitation. Have people move from station to station on their own, exploring what practices work for them and settling into being alone with God. You may also wish to spend some time moving from practice to practice as a group.

When I have worked with a spiritual practices experience of various stations, it has been rich and engaging for youth and leaders. Hold this kind of intentional gathering in a beautiful space where attention has been paid to detail and there is space for a variety of responses to God. Many of the practices in this book can be used in a station-based practices experience. It's important to have clear and simple written instructions at each station that outline the practice and make it easy to understand and follow.

Below is a method for organizing a spiritual practices experience. You may choose a theme to work with and relate all the practices to that theme, or you may create a variety of practices based on the needs of the youth you work with.

The example below works through the process of setting up a practices experience related to the theme *There is a time.* When you set up your own practices experience, remember to spend some time focusing on how the space will be set up.

Practices Experience Example

 Set the theme and intention. For example:

To introduce a variety of new practices to the youth participants, working with the theme of There is a time *(Ecclesiastes 3). Opening will include sharing the scripture passage with projected images; then introduction of the practice time (see below). The practice will end with calling all participants to the central table and closing with a prayer, allowing youth to participate if they wish.*

INTENTION	PRACTICE	SUPPLIES
To encourage participants to experience prayer through movement.	A Time to Move practice (see page 161)	An area for people to move around in. Three stations set up, each with an instruction sheet. Wall space or chair to hold the instruction sheet at each station.
To encourage participants to actively embody their prayers, saying them aloud.	A time to be silent and a time to speak: Wailing Wall practice (see page 169)	Wall with written instructions posted. A Christ candle on a table nearby.
To encourage participants to pray through a Biblical story or image using ancient and modern icons.	A time to see the story: Praying with Icons (see page 90)	Large table with a chair at each corner (for each of four stations). Place a variety of icons on the table and allow people to choose one to work with. Instruction sheet on tables at each station. Candle at each station.

There are no limits to how and where you can set up a spiritual practices experience. You could set it up outside or inside. Ideally, there would be a central table for gathering around with small tables or areas set up in the rest of the space for individuals to work at. Make sure the room is large enough to allow for some personal space around each station. Have all supplies laid out at each station, along with a candle or two and an instruction sheet. Have the space prepared (candles lit, adequate seating, soft music playing) before the youth arrive. Gather outside the space and introduce the practices before entering the space. Offer the following instructions.

We are inviting you into a time that is just for you, a time for you to rest and renew yourself, a time for you to slow down and listen and experience and explore many different ways to pray. Your world is a busy loud and full place. Tonight we are asking that you try experiencing life in a different way. We have set up the room with different practice stations and we'd ask that you spend the next hour going from station to station, doing the practices and exploring which practices work for you. If you find a station that you wish to stay at, please do so. It's okay if you only make it to one station, or if you go to all of them.

Remember you are doing this time of practice on your own in a room with other people. We ask that you hold the silence when you are in the room. When the practices time is over, we will ring a bell and ask you to gather around the central table after you finish the practice you are working on. There is no need to rush away from what you are doing – we will wait for you to finish. We will end with a short prayer of reflection.

We will now enter into a time of prayer together.

Invite youth to enter the space in small groups. Allow time for people to sink into being in the room. Typically I have the spiritual practices sessions run from one to two hours, and I allow time for people to remain in the space following the closing prayer if they wish. It's important that all those present participate, including leaders and those who have set up the space. I have often been astounded at how long the practice sessions have gone. We assume that youth have short attention spans but I've witnessed youth literally lose themselves in the practices. It's always with reluctance that I ring the bell to end the practices as I know some of the youth could just keep going.

Close the evening with a prayer (below) once all have gathered around the central table. You may wish to have a longer service to end, but keep in mind that people have been worshipping in their own way for the past hour or so. Keeping the closing brief can be a helpful and congruent way to end the practice.

Loving God, thank you for this time to focus on you and our connection with you. We are grateful for this place and this time to be in a community of friends praying together. In the stillness we seek you. In the stillness we bring all that we are. In the stillness we open to your presence. Amen.

INTEGRATING A PRACTICES SESSION INTO A SERVICE

This is an example of how you might integrate a practices session into a youth service. The focus of the practices experience will be *Savouring God through the senses*.

 Set up the following practices: Tasting Life (page 95), Savouring Scent (page 96), Candle Meditation (page 83), Chillin' to Sound (page 98), Water Blessing (page 103), and Creation Prayer (page 78). Set the central table with a feast of food (such as grapes, apples, chocolate), some flowers, and a Christ Candle.

Ask someone to play a simple drumbeat at the beginning and the end of the service.

Song: Choose a song

 Opening Words (leader)

Take some time and space. Lay down burdens, breathe out stress, release pressure, shed some layers, go to pieces, patch it up. Take some time and space. Arrive well, enter silence, breathe in life, embrace peace, gaze on Christ. Take some time and space. You are loved, you are free, you are safe, you are part of God. Take some time and space to breathe into the presence of God in this room. Breathe in deeply and release. Breathe in life and breathe out stress. Breathe in deeply, breathe out struggle. Breathe in deeply, breathe out worry. Breathe in life, breathe out scattered. Breath of life. Breathe in spirit of life.

 Song: *All Who Hunger* (Voices United)

 I have come so that you may have life in abundance. Delight in the world. You are alive to savour earthly delights.
Jesus said, "I came that they might have life, and might have it abundantly." (John 10:10)

Personal Practice

 Invite people to explore the Savouring God practices you have set up around the room. Allow 15 minutes or more for people to intentionally and slowly experience the practices.

Begin the practices after some moments of silence together.

Have the drumbeat call people back to the circle. Then share the food together.

This is a table set to be together. An abundance of flowers, grapes, apples, and chocolate.

As you share the food we ask you to share your response to these questions:

- *How do you savour God?*
- *How do you savour the abundance of life?*

Pass the food around, serving one another casually, and share the responses to the questions.

Closing Prayer

Oh Great Savourer, oh Spirit of Life, our mouths are filled by your light, our eyes take in the fullness of your beauty, our inner energy is full of you, our ears delight in hearing all you name good, our noses smell the richness of you. Oh One who delights in our delight, oh One who savours us, may we savour all the great goodness given us.

Chant or Song to close

IN CLOSING

Given the wide variety of activities and choices that youth have in their everyday lives, it is important to recognize their need for choice in their response to God. Choose practices that will engage many different styles and levels of faith journeying.

I urge you to use the scriptures in your practice times, as they hold an integral place in the Christian faith. Scripture may be a window that allows some youth to come more deeply into faith. I encourage you to use sources from modern-day prophets also – writers, artists, musicians, and poets. They can sometimes speak more clearly to youth than scripture can.

Engage in practices from other faith traditions, borrowing (with acknowledgment and respect) practices that can work to pull people toward God. Explain where you found the practice from another tradition, how it is used, and how you will be adapting it for your practice. Remember that each youth you minister to will have a unique style, preference, and path to God. Your task is to provide the experience, the opportunity to open into an encounter with God.

As all the pieces of building a life of faith come together, we see that many parts make up the whole and create a home for the faith of youth to grow and live.

In reading through these pages you have perhaps begun to imagine ways you could encourage a time of spiritual practice in your own ministry context. It's time to put aside all the words and just breathe deeply into your own potential as a leader. Take a look at how you practice in your own life, and look ahead at the glorious possibilities. What an incredible gift and responsibility to be one who can offer youth an opening to the Divine. Now it's time to practice with intention.

 Wild passionate God; eyes, ears, body, being, heart open to you. Open to experience. Open to mystery. Guide us so we may learn more of you. Teach us our way to be in your wild passionate way. In the name of the One for whom we are named, we pray. Amen.

YOUTH PRACTICES

Reach out and hold on to one another and God.
Seek peace and connection with the Divine wherever you go.
Show that connection as every turn of the road of your life unfolds.

Part II of this resource contains practices that engage youth through the use of senses, words, visual arts, crafts, movement, service, and community. The practices are meant to pull us to unfolding into a more integrated and holistic approach to our faith.

Take all you have engaged with in your life so far, all that you have engaged with in this resource, and claim your role as the leader you are meant to be. Continue to enter into the practices with the youth in your ministry programs. Use what is here as guide, adapt where you need to, create your own practices where you are called to do so. Encounter and welcome openness and surprise in the flowing river of your life.

CHAPTER 4

enGaGING THE senses

God is the impulse to laugh. ~ Rumi

The practices in this chapter invite you to engage your senses and pay close attention to the connection with God that comes when we focus on our capacities of sense.

Mindfulness may be defined as noticing and paying attention in the present moment. It's about nurturing each moment with acceptance and gratitude and being fully alive and aware of what is happening now – what is.

We are acculturated to look to the future: Where are you going? What will you do? What are your plans? We also live partly in the past, in a dream of remembering, unable to let go of people, situations, hurts, and joys. In reality, all we have is God's gift of the present moment. Our task is to figure out how to live our life fully right now.

Being born into an affluent culture has afforded us tremendous choice and possibility, for health and harm. The mindfulness practices of breathing and noticing can be helpful in calming, centring, and bringing to awareness how the body carries stress. By being mindful we can consciously choose things that will bring us into life in all its fullness.

The practice below is a meditation on awareness. Practice in a group in a space with room for movement and if possible windows to the outside world, or do the practice outside.

 Ask youth to find a space and sit or stand comfortably with their eyes closed. Read the opening prayer aloud, in a gentle and meditative way, leaving silence between the lines for personal contemplation.

MINDFULNESS I

 I breathe in deeply.

Over and over, the rhythm of my breath carries me. I don't have to force anything.

Spirit, you are my breath, inside my breath, the rhythm that gives me life.

I breathe into this present moment. I notice my breathing.

I give thanks for this gift of life that is this present moment.

I open my ears.

I am aware of the sounds that are around me. I notice them in this present moment, listening to whatever sound comes to me. I give thanks for this gift of sound in this present moment, reminder of life all around. (Allow time for exploration of sound.)

I open my eyes.

My gaze falls on something in my range of sight. I notice the thing I am watching – its beauty, simplicity, function, and form. I notice in this present moment the beauty of all parts of the world around me. I give thanks for the gift of sight in this present moment, reminder of the life of the world all around me. (Allow time for exploration of sight.)

I move in the world. I feel my feet touch the ground, connecting with all that is around me. In this present moment I notice how I am feeling. I accept it. I move my body in this space around me, filling up space, moving, shaking, dancing, and twirling. I am filling up this space in this present moment. (Allow time for people to explore the space with their movements.)

I stop to a still place and notice how my body feels in stillness. (Allow time to notice.)

I have this present moment. It is all I really have.

I breathe deeply, bringing myself back to the space where I am alive.

I raise my hands and thank God for this present moment. I acknowl-
edge that it is all I really have. I breathe deeply into this present
moment.
Amen.

After the present moment practice, invite youth to talk in small groups about what focusing on the present moment was like.

Seeing, hearing, tasting, smelling, and touching are all ways we take in life. If all of life is holy and infused with the presence of God, then our very senses are a direct way into that Presence. Often we function in automatic pilot mode, not noticing what our senses take in. When senses are engaged in an intentional way, when we pay attention, we are practicing God's presence in the mystery and wonder of the senses we are gifted with. Open yourself to seeing, hearing, tasting, smelling, and touching, and God and the world will become more alive to you.

 I am alive. I am seeing, hearing, breathing, touching, moving,
tasting, loving.

I am alive.

I am seeing God, hearing God, breathing God, touching God,
moving God, tasting God, loving God, living God.

I am alive.

I know that God is seeing me, hearing me, breathing me, touching
me, moving me, loving me.

I am alive.

Every time I seek, I am found; every time I speak, I am heard; every time I breathe, I am breathed; every time I touch, I am known; every time I move, I am moved; every time I love, I am loved. Every time I know God, I am alive.
Amen.

MINDFULNESS II

The world is truly a lofty beautiful place, with God in every crack and crevice; where, if we pay attention, we can fall into a still, humble, and prayerful space. The world glows with the consciousness of God, and noticing is all it takes to make Holiness real in our lives.

This is a practice of going out into the world and savouring everything that comes across our path, opening all our senses to what is. This is a practice of stepping out of our dwelling place and taking a walk in the cathedral of the world.

 Send youth out for a walk tasked with paying attention. Tell them to look around, notice things, look at whatever catches their eye for a while. Spend time studying a leaf on a tree, or a dandelion growing out of a crack in the sidewalk. Really notice one small thing and spend some time in that space. Ask them to come back after their walk and share one thing they noticed and what drew them to it. This sharing of the world becomes a prayer.

CREATION PRAYER

This practice invites people to take a close look at something from the natural world and then write a prayer about the experience. You can do this practice inside with a number of items from nature (pine cones, rocks, feathers, old bird's nest, driftwood, etc.) set on a cental table, or you may go outside.

 Have an envelope containing a piece of paper, pencil, the directions, and the Psalm (see page 80) available for each participant. Before beginning the task, share in the opening prayer below. Hand out the envelopes and allow at least 15 minutes for the practice. It is helpful to call people back with the ringing of a bell or prayer bowl. Invite people to put their written prayer work into a bowl and then invite each person to select one and share it aloud, without further comment from anyone. End with a repetition of the opening prayer.

 Creator God, artist God, building, moving, and living God. Your colours collide in the beauty that is all around us in air, earth, water, light, and one another. Be with us as we pay close attention to your creation and what it means for us.
Amen.

Hand out envelopes. Ask people to read and follow the directions in the envelope.

Creation Prayer

Choose one item from the table that speaks to you. Take it with you and find a quiet place to sit. Read the following Psalm scripture while holding the piece of creation in your hand. Notice it in detail. What is miraculous about it? What about it speaks to you?

Or

As you are in the natural world outside, walk around for a little while until your eyes and heart rest on one piece of creation, tiny or big. Find a quiet place to sit and be in its presence. Read the following Psalm scripture as you keep noticing and paying attention to your particular piece of nature. Notice it in detail. What is miraculous about this piece of creation? What draws you?

Then

When you are ready, use the paper and pencil provided and write or draw a poem of thanks, perhaps focusing on the piece of nature that you chose to pay attention to. When you are called by the bell, take the poem back and put it in the bowl on the centre table. Your poem or picture will be chosen by someone else in the group and they will share the words or image with the whole group, without naming who created the work.

Psalm 148

Praise the Blessed One!
Give praise from the heavens,
   and from all ends of
    the earth!
Give praise all you angels,
   angels of earth and of heaven!

Give praise sun and moon,
   give praise, all you shining stars!
Give praise, all universes,
   the whole cosmos of Creation!

Praise the Blessed One!
   For through Love all was created
And firmly fixed for ever and ever;
   Yes, the pattern of creation
    Was established.
Give praise to the Beloved,
   all the earth,
   all that swim in the deep,
And all the winged ones in the air!

Give praise all mountains and hills,
   all trees and all minerals!
Give praise all four-legged
   and all that creep on the ground!

Leaders of the nations and all peoples,
   young and old,
Give praise! Unite together in all
   your diversity,
   that peace and harmony might
   flourish on earth!

Let all people praise the Beloved,
   who is exalted in heaven and
    on earth;
   whose glory is above heaven
    and earth.

For all are called to be friends,
   companions to the true Friend,
   giving their lives joyfully as
    co-creators and people
    of peace!
Praises be to the Blessed One,
   the very breath of our breath,
   the very Heart of our heart!

Nan Merrill[1]

PRAYER TABLE FOR THE YOUTH ROOM

Throughout history, people have responded to God's call by creating beautiful places, where the glory of the space reflects the glory of God. Being in a beautiful space can remind us that God's beauty is all around us, sustaining us.

Your youth room can reflect the lives and interests of the people in it and the beauty you yearn for. Spend time thinking about the space and how to set it up. Work to create a simple and beautiful space that youth will be drawn to.

 The prayer table is meant to be an object of focus and reverence. Create a prayer table with the youth as a way of beginning your year together. Cover a low table with a beautiful piece of cloth and set in the middle of the room or along one of the walls. You may wish to use a prayer cloth that the youth create at the beginning of each youth group year (see page 140) Your prayer table could include the Christ Candle (see page 84), symbols related to the theme of the current week; a place for a God box (see page 135), or a place for photos of those who need prayers (youth bring these in). This prayer table could also be a place for the beauty of the natural world to be present indoors (rocks, feathers, flowers in a vase).

Allow youth to create the space with you; their ownership will be much greater if they have input. It's also important to use the prayer table each time your group meets. Use it even if the only thing you do is to light a candle and bring God to mind. This way, you are engaging ritual – sacred practices that remind us who we are and to whom we belong. Many of the practices in this book have the potential to become rituals for your group. Use the prayer table in the youth room to pull people toward God, one another, and ritual.

© Doris Kizinna

© Doris Kizinna

PRAYER NICHE

Prayer niches are found in many religions. In Roman Catholic churches you can see them as altars along the sides of the church; in mosques they are often on a wall facing Mecca. Buddhist temples have small altars set up with offerings for the Buddha and the ancestors. Prayer niches may be found in homes as sacred spaces in which to pray or meditate.

You could create a prayer niche in your youth room as a private place to pray and meditate during youth meetings or at other times. A small prayer niche can be created by attaching a box, ideally made of wood, to the wall. Make the box a focal point for youth to stop at. Have the youth decorate it as they would something sacred, perhaps adding pictures for things that need prayer and a candle (be careful with the wood). You may wish to put the niche behind a divider to allow for privacy, and add a cushion or chair to sit on. Encourage youth to use the niche for their personal times of reflection.

One of the prayer niches pictured above is simply a large bowl filled with stones, a singing bowl, and a cross placed on a small table. It is a place to stop and contemplate, and has been used in a home.

CANDLE MEDITATION

This is an individual practice that can be part of a practice stations experience. A simple set-up of a candle and the directions below on a table with a chair in front of it is all that is required.

Candle Meditation

Sit comfortably in the chair. Spend some time focusing on the candle before you, breathing deeply. Cast your gaze into the depth of the flame. Repeat a phrase you make up (or use one below) over and over as you seek to understand the constant energy of God's presence, like the candle flame, in your life.

God, your light sustains me

Jesus, you are the Light of the World

Spirit, you are present in flame and energy

© Doris Kizinna

CHRIST CANDLE

Candles have been used over the centuries to provide warmth and light, gather people, and symbolize light in a dark world. Often Christian churches have a candle on the altar to represent the light of Christ present with us.

A Christ candle can act as a focal point in a youth ministry context. If you begin every youth meeting by lighting the candle and saying a few words about gathering in the light of Christ, you set the stage for a particular kind of gathering – one where people follow the teachings of Christ, celebrate life in all its fullness, and are bound in its diversity by the light.

 You can make a group Christ candle or individual ones. Visit a candle-making or craft store and gather supplies to make either poured hot wax mould candles or rolled beeswax candles. Take your group to a beach or park and gather small stones, shells, or beach glass to use in the candle making process. If you are creating one large candle, have each person add a stone or shell to the wax while saying aloud their prayer for the life of the group. If you are making individual candles, add a shell or stone to each other's candle as a symbol of group unity and connection. Each person can etch words or symbols about their hopes for the year onto a piece of wax and contribute it to the melted wax that will form the candle.

Pour the melted wax into a mould. A milk carton filled with ice cubes is a low tech mould. The ice cubes melt as the wax hardens and leave interesting holes and rivulets in the texture of the candle. You could choose to use the candle you make as the Christ candle in your youth room, or have youth take their candles home as a reminder of their fellow youth group members who offer prayers for them.

aDVeNT caNDLes

The Latin word *advent* means "the coming." Advent is the time in the Christian faith that we remember the birth of Jesus. Advent begins on the Sunday nearest November 30 and lasts four Sundays, ending the Sunday before Christmas. Each Sunday of Advent carries a different theme: faith, hope, joy, love. There is often a ceremonial lighting of Advent candles each week.

You can get creative in making an Advent candle centre for your youth room. The candles don't need to be the traditional, liturgically correct three purple, one pink, and one white Christ candle set in greenery. Get creative! Let youth decide how their Advent wreath – a visual reminder of the story of the coming of Jesus – will look.

During Advent, you may wish to have a short weekly service to reflect on the coming of Jesus. Below are scripture suggestions and questions for each of the Sundays of Advent.

First Sunday of Advent: Hope

 Light one candle to symbolize Hope.

 Read Isaiah 60:2–3

Where do you see hope in your own life?
How do you see that Jesus may be a hope for the world?

 Prayer: Hopeful God, we thank you for the feeling of hope we find in… (list the things and places your group finds hope in).
Amen.

Second Sunday of Advent: Peace

 Light two candles – Hope and Peace.

 Read Matthew 5:9

Have newspaper stories about peace (and lack of it) on the table around the Advent candles. Ask each person to read one story and share something about where peace is needed. Close with a prayer for peace.

 Prayer: Peacemaker God, we are called to be peacemakers. Help us remember... (list the places around the world) and to pray, act, and live always for peace.

Third Sunday: Joy

 Light three candles – Hope, Peace, and Joy.

 Read Isaiah 35:10

When do you feel joy?
Where do you feel joy?
How do you bring joy to others?
What joy do you feel about the birth of Jesus?

 Prayer: Joyful God, we find joy in ... (list when/where/how your group finds joy). Thanks for joy deep in our hearts.
Amen.

Fourth Sunday: Love

 Light four candles – Hope, Peace, Joy, and Love.

 Read Isaiah 9:6–7

What does being loved mean to you?
What can you share about the love of God in your life?

 Prayer: God of Love, for love we are grateful, for love our lives are fuller, for love we live. We find love in ... (list the things and places your group finds love in). Thank you for the love surrounding us. Amen.

Christmas Eve

 Light all five candles.

 Read Luke 1:76–79 and Luke 2:1–20

What does it mean for you that Jesus was born into this world?

 Prayer: This is a special night of remembering when hope, peace, joy, and love came into the world in the form of a baby. We are thankful that we can remember Jesus and his life among us and all that means.
Amen.

VISUAL ART GALLERY

Visual imagery can speak to the heart. Creating visual imagery connects us with the Creator and draws us closer to understanding one another and the gifts we bring. You may wish to create spaces in your worship area/youth room that sing with the creativity of members of the program.

This practice invites youth in the congregation to work on an art project together. Have a theme to work with: God's love, what happens when we die, things that pull you closer to God. For people who choose not to paint or draw, suggest writing poetry, or provide cameras and then have the techies among you put together a slide presentation that can be shown in the gallery.

 Choose a room and set it up as you would an art gallery. Group artwork together thematically, print out the poems and mount them on the walls among the artwork, have the slide images looping. The gallery could be open on a Sunday following church and if possible during the week. You may wish to leave the gallery in place while your group creates another themed show.

These works of art are an intentional practice for the youth who create them, but will also be a practice for those who experience them as they open to God's presence through the work of others. You could leave a comment book or box in the gallery for feedback. Create a handout that reflects on the theme of the exhibit and perhaps offers questions and a practice to engage in while viewing the gallery. This practice is a great way for youth to share their own ministry with other members of the congregation.

SLIDe SHOW

Showing a slide show of images with music playing can be a calming and meditative practice. Many groups will have access to an LCD projector and a screen; in fact many churches are using them instead of bulletins. Using images when scripture is being read enhances the experience. A spiritual practice can be based on images also.

Most youth are quite familiar with putting together a PowerPoint presentation, which is the basic format used in creating a presentation of images. Have them put it together with you, or let them create their own as a way for them to be fully involved. Use photos that members of your youth group or congregation have taken, or free Internet images from downloading sites.

 Choose a theme for the slide show (e.g., light, darkness, war and peace, images of Jesus). Set up a large screen and loop the images so that they play continuously (with at least five seconds on each image), and run the images throughout the whole spiritual practice. You could also watch the images once or twice through and then have some conversation about them and the theme you have connected them with.

If you are using the slide show as part of a spiritual practices experience, it will be helpful to have the following outline for the practice available in front of the screen for people to check out.

A Time to See

Focus on each image as it comes on the screen. Paying attention to these images is a form of prayer. They will speak to you in a variety of ways. As each picture passes by, say the words *God is here* silently, or use a mantra that you choose yourself.

ICONS

Christian icons have historically been of stories from scripture. In the early church, many people couldn't read or didn't have access to the scripture texts, so the icons were a reminder of the stories of faith. Today icons are still used extensively in the Eastern and Orthodox churches as well as in other religions. An icon is also a way for the artist to worship and pay homage to their faith and the stories within that faith. The use of icons is an integral part of the worship experience at Taizé, an ecumenical community in France, whose members use them as a way to tell stories with few words.

© Public Domain

The icon on the left is of Jesus with St. Mina and is prominent at the Taizé community. The image of Jesus with his arm around his disciple suggests seeing Jesus as our friend as a way into the story.

☛ The icon practice involves spending time in prayer with the icon. Set the icon on a table with a candle, pen and paper, and the following instructions for an individual practice or a spiritual practices experience station. You may use the icon pictured here or another of your choice.

Icons

Sit comfortably on the chair and breathe deeply in and out a few
times, stilling your mind.

Focus on the icon before you.

What do you notice about the icon?

How do you see your connection with the life of Jesus?

What does it mean to you to be a follower of Jesus?

What would you say to Jesus if he were a trusted friend in your life
today?

Take a pen and a slip of paper and write down some of your thoughts
on who Jesus is to you.

WORKS OF aRT

Any work of art can be inspirational if you really pay attention and seek
to understand it. The way of the artist is to manifest creativity within in
order to have an impact on the lives of other people through their witness to the work.

This art practice could be done in an art gallery or with pictures from
books. Choose a specific painting to pray with and notice what the work
of the artist is saying to you. Give people the steps listed below on a
piece of paper to take with them on their walk through the gallery, or
have beside them as they look through art books. Have each person
choose one painting that speaks to them. Once they have chosen their
piece, they follow the steps below.

Praying with Works of Art

1. **Stillness.** Stop in front of the work of art. Breathe deeply. Calm your mind.

2. **Noticing.** Pay attention to the details. Notice colours, the space the piece takes up, the little things. Just spend time taking in the details of the work. Where does your eye most want to stay? What feelings or thoughts do you notice about the images you are taking in?

3. **Responding.** Offer a prayer of thanksgiving for the artist and their gift. Let the image wash over you in this prayer. Bring whatever thoughts or issues that have arisen to your prayer. Speak your prayer aloud, ask for what you need and give thanks for what you are grateful for, letting the images continue to wash through you and your prayer.

4. **Stillness.** End the way you began. Breathe deeply. Calm your heart and mind.

5. **Acknowledge.** As you leave the painting, recognize the relationship you now have with this work of art. You will never see it the same way again. It has meaning for you.

Once the group members have finished their reflections, take a tour of all the works of art chosen, stopping briefly at each piece and taking it in. There is no need to recap each person's prayer. Just take in each of the works of art as a simple and beautiful response.

WaTCHING FILMS

Most youth watch films regularly and are plugged in to what the latest, greatest movie out there is. Films can initiate and stimulate conversation and reflection. Those with appropriate themes and content can move people into understanding more about themselves, their community, and their connection with God.

I remember taking my senior youth group to see *Dead Man Walking*, a particularly stirring film about a young man on death row in the USA. As I sat in the theatre, I heard some in my group weeping. As we left the theatre, I was faced with a group of youth who had been so moved and so stunned by the film that they were all ready to burst into tears. Instead of just heading home, we went to a café and debriefed, talking about the film's impact on us and how that story connected with our own lives. Conversation then shifted to lighter topics, laughter came again, and we moved from darkness to light. We ended the night with a prayer for prisoners on death row around the world, sending them love and light.

Films that stir us to compassion, action, joy, or rage are films that I would consider watching as a spiritual practice. A film can give us the gift of perspective and a message that we need to hear. The key is for the leader to relate the film to the spiritual lives of the youth. See resources page for websites with film suggestions.

 Choose a film that you have seen yourself and that you think would bring people to a place of understanding themselves and God's world in a more intimate way. Choose a film that is appropriate for the age group that you are working with, paying attention to ratings. Avoid films with inappropriate language and graphic scenes. It's also important that you have official permission to watch the film. Many congregations or church offices will hold copyright to show films on-site, since it's against copyright law to show movies at a youth group meeting without copyright permission.

Set up a comfortable and safe space to watch the film in. Often a film will move us to tears and having a safe place to be when our hearts are so stirred is vital. Again, as with all practice, intention is important. Reflection following the film will help give meaning to the experience.

Introduce the film by giving a rough storyline and an idea of what to expect. Ask people to pay attention to their reactions to the film: what moved them most, what character they most related to, how they saw God's presence.

Offer a ten-minute break following the film's conclusion. Invite people to get a drink, have a break, walk outside, and formulate a one sentence review of the film. Regroup, share the one sentence reviews, and spend some time in open conversation relating to the three questions posed at the beginning of the film. (What moved you most in the film? What character did you most relate to? How did you see God's presence in the film?) Spend some time in conversation, invite those who haven't spoken or contributed to do so.

End the reflection with a closing prayer where people are offered the opportunity to use their own voice to pray their own prayer.

TaSTING LIFe

This practice is ideal for a spiritual practices experience but may also be used as an individual practice.

 Set out three bowls of food items to taste (honey, sugar, salt, vinegar, cherry tomatoes, pieces of orange, etc.). Choose items that have a pleasant or noticeable taste and place only a small amount of the food in each bowl. Place small spoons or stir sticks beside each bowl so that people can easily help themselves. Set the bowls, a candle, and a blindfold on a table and place a chair in front of the station. Have people read the sheet before they close their eyes or blindfold themselves.

Tasting Life

Notice the bowls on the table.

Close your eyes or put on the blindfold.

Taste the item in one bowl savouring what you taste. Pause, breathe deeply, and then taste the next thing. You may need to use the spoon to take the food from the bowls.

Notice the difference in the tastes. Savour each of the tastes.
When you have finished the tasting practice, offer a prayer of gratitude for the gift of taste, and for all the foods that you love to eat.

SAVOURING SCENT

This practice is ideal for a spiritual practices experience but could also be used as an individual practice.

Set out on a table a few small bowls containing items that have a distinct yet pleasant scent. You may use some drops of essential oil (lavender, grapefruit, cedar), a cut up orange, a highly perfumed rose, vinegar, ground coffee, or cinnamon sticks. Provide the written outline beside the bowls to direct people through the practice.

Savouring Scent

Make yourself comfortable in the chair and take some deep breaths in and out. Notice the bowls on the table. Pick up each one in turn and sniff deeply. Pause for some time between each bowl.

As you savour the aroma in each bowl, what thoughts or images arise with the scent? Perhaps the scent reminds you of something, maybe you are drawn to it, maybe it's not your favourite aroma. Just sit and notice.

Once you have savoured each scent, sit in silence, then smell again the scent that you were most drawn to. When you are finished the practice, offer a silent prayer of gratitude for the gift of smell.

Hearing

© istockphoto.com

This is a picture of a singing bowl. My singing bowl is a 100-year-old bowl from Nepal that my grandmother gave me. It has a very special deep and rich sound. Tibetan singing bowls are used in the practices of Tibetan Buddhism. When played the right way these bowls do indeed sing. They can be struck on the side for a deep rich note or they can be played by dragging the mallet around the outside rim of the bowl to produce a continuous sound. They are now used worldwide within many different faith traditions and for relaxation and meditation outside of religious practice and are readily available for purchase. I have played this singing bowl at many youth events as a way to begin a worship service or a spiritual practices experience. People are spellbound by its sound.

The sound of the singing bowl is one way to engage the sense of hearing. Bells, chimes, circle singing, sound improvisation, soft meditative music, and loud engulfing music are other ways to introduce sound into ministry with youth.

Hearing is a very important sense for us to pay attention to in creating practices for youth. Youth crave sound in the forms of music, conversation, and noise of many kinds. It fills the spaces in their lives with excitement and energy.

CHILLIN' TO SOUND

Use this as a station at a spiritual practices experience or as an individual practice.

 Set up a listening station with a comfy chair or a big pile of pillows. Have a small table set up nearby with a candle and the instructions for this practice (below) on it. Load onto an mp3 player an instrumental song that expresses the beauty of sound.

Savouring Sound

Find a comfortable spot on the chair or in the pillows to relax. Hook yourself up to the mp3 player and close your eyes. Breathe deeply as you settle into the space and relax. Pay attention to the music that you hear and let thoughts and images flow as you listen. Notice how you feel.

Once you have finished listening to the piece, sit and imagine what your life would be like without the gift of hearing. What are you grateful for in the gifts of hearing and sound? Say the words *thank you* out loud to yourself three times as you rise to leave.

LAUGHTER

Shared laughter is holy medicine and can bring contentment, healing, and a sense of belonging. There is a yoga practice that involves a group of people simply beginning to laugh. Suddenly everyone is laughing, at themselves and one another. Muscles relax and a sense of well-being ensues. There are laughter yoga clubs around North America where you can go and practice.

Life brings struggle, and laughing in the midst of it is a way to get through it. My father has Alzheimer's disease and often in the midst of times when he makes mistakes and loses his way we all just begin to laugh, my father included. We laugh at the difficulty of the situation, and at our ability to see the humour in the fact that this man just put his shoes on the wrong feet. We laugh as a response to pain and grief. Laughing and including him in our laughter brings some lightness to the situation. We remember we are still alive and able to love despite struggle and hardship.

Some people have a gift of being able to make people laugh easily; it's great to have a couple of them on hand at all times! Generally our culture is one that doesn't laugh all that much – perhaps this says something about our way of being in the world. But however and whenever we do it, laughing changes us. It changes our chemical makeup through movement and relaxation. Great spiritual teachers such as His Holiness the Dalai Lama and Bishop Desmond Tutu are said to be people of laughter.

Laughter is deeply healing; it reduces stress and brings us into our bodies. Below are some ways to infuse the spiritual practice of laughter into your ministry with youth:

- *Have a comedy night where people simply try and make others laugh in ways that are respectful and don't make fun of others. Remember that laughing at someone is very different from laughing with someone. Be aware and set very clear guidelines about what kind of jokes are appropriate.*

- *Ask people to start to laugh, from deep in their bellies. See how long the laughter goes, and how contagious it becomes, and how forced laughter can quickly become real laughter.*

- *Invite a clown or comedian or a laughter yoga instructor to your youth group.*

- *Mostly the best laughter moments can't be planned or organized; they just happen, and a deep belly laugh is a spontaneous response. Don't be afraid to open your mouth and laugh at situations and at the joy that you feel. Sharing a deep belly laugh is one of the best ways to build community and connection with others. It builds confidence and self-expression.*

- *Seek to understand that laughing is a response to life. Laugh out loud in your prayers, laugh within, laugh at yourself, laugh with gratitude for this marvellous gift!*

GReeTING THe DaY

People around the world use the sun's rising and setting as a way to greet or to end their day. There are dances, prayers and rituals surrounding the sun's reliable, mysterious, and life-giving presence.

Sunrise can be a magical time of stillness and peace where people feel deep connection with the Divine. When was the last time you got up to watch the sun rise? This group or individual practice is especially good to do in the summer when the day's warmth will help make the experience something to savour. It is a great practice during a retreat or at a summer camp as a way to build community.

Find a place to greet the sun that works for your group. Bring with you a small breakfast feast. Allow yourself enough time to get there and set up the space before the others arrive (before the sun is up). Share in a prayer before the sun rises; watch the sun rise, then pray again after sunrise. Follow with a breakfast snack or feast that you have brought with you. You may wish to bring some beautiful music to play on a portable player while the sun is rising, remembering to allow stillness also. If it is a special day in the life of someone in your group (such as a birthday), the experience of beginning the special day while watching the sunrise can be meaningful and can build the gathered community.

Prayer before sunrise

Creator God, we wait in the darkness, knowing the light coming. As we stand here in the beauty of the coming morning light, we let go of the night that was. There is stillness as the world waits for the light. We ask to know your presence in all things dark and light, and in waiting for a new day to break.

Watch in stillness as the sun comes up.

Prayer after sunrise

Creator God, the sun is up and life feels new again. We are standing in this light, looking at the same sun that people all around the world share, the same sun that has shone down on every being throughout history. We think of our brothers and sisters around the world who greet the day from riverbanks, on mountaintops, in backyards, in cars commuting to work, running on the beach, or looking out of kitchen windows, all paying attention to your gifts. We think now of the precious day to come, all of it ours to explore and live into. We

are thankful for another day of life, for another chance. We are in
awe of all the wonders of creation and we give humble thanks. For
food in a world where many are without, we give grateful thanks.
Amen.

Share in breakfast.

TOUCHING STRONG aND SOLID LOVe

 Have a basket of beautiful rocks (purchase or gather enough for one for
each person) on a table with a candle and the following instructions.

Touching the Rock-Solid Love of God

Rocks remind us of

- The age and beauty of the earth
- The mystery of creation
- The solid and strong love of God
- The meaning of forever
- Perfection

Choose a rock from the basket that speaks to you. Notice its shape,
form, and colour. Hold it tightly in your hand for some moments. Contemplate how the rock is like the solid and strong love of God that is
with you always.

Take the rock with you, keeping it with you until you find the right
person to pass it on to. Give it to someone as a reminder of the
strong, solid, timeless love of God. Pass it on.

ANOINTING WITH WATER OR OIL

This is a practice to use as people enter a spiritual practices experience or a worship service.

Set out on a table a large clear plastic or glass bowl half full of water and a small bowl of oil for the purpose of anointing. Water and oil have been used in the Christian tradition over time to baptize, heal, and bless. Traditionally, the one presiding at a service will be the one anointing, baptizing, and blessing, but in this practice people will individually offer themselves a blessing through anointing themselves with oil and water.

This is a practice of remembrance of when we were blessed with water and oil at our baptism, confirmation, or other service. For those who haven't been baptized, it can be seen as a simple act of blessing themselves.

Place the following directions and a few towels for people to use after the practice at the station with the bowl of water and oil.

Water Blessing

And when Jesus had been baptized, just as he came up from the water, suddenly the heavens were opened to him and he saw the Spirit of God descending like a dove and alighting on him. And a voice from heaven said, "This is my Son, the Beloved, with whom I am well pleased." Matthew 3:16–17

And let everyone who is thirsty come.
Let anyone who wishes take the water of life as a gift. Revelation 22:17

Take a moment and stand before the bowl of water. Remember how water blesses your life. Water gives you life.

This water is a symbol of your belonging to God and will quench all you are thirsting for. God proclaimed to Jesus, "In you I am well pleased." God proclaims that about you as well: "In you I am well pleased."

Dip your hand into the bowl of water and drip water on your other hand or on your face, blessing your body. You may wish to make the sign of the cross with the water on your hand or face to remind you that you belong to God and that God is pleased in your simply being.

Oil Blessing

You anoint my head with oil; my cup overflows. Psalm 23:5

Take a moment and stand before the small bowl of oil. This is sacred oil that nourishes, sustains, soothes, comforts, and heals us. Remember how you belong to God.

Dip your finger into the bowl and anoint your own hand or your forehead with a small amount of oil. You may wish to make the sign of the cross, or just smooth oil into your skin, marking yourself as blessed. You anoint your head with oil and your cup overflows.

PRAYER TO END THE CHAPTER

Holy Presence, who stirred me into being, who created all that lives, to you I give thanks. I am alive to what I see, hear, touch, taste, and love. I see your presence, oh God, in my actions, in how I love, and in all I seek. I am alive. When I see, I understand. When I listen, I am heard. When I breathe, I live. When I touch, I am known. When I love, I am blessed. Amen.

Merrill, Nan. *Psalms for Praying, An Invitation to Wholeness* (Continuum International Publishing Group, New York, 2007) p. 294. Copyright 2000, 2006. Reprinted by permission of the Continuum International Publishing Group.

CHAPTER 5

WORD PRACTICES

Preach the gospel at all times –
If necessary, use words. ~ St. Francis of Assisi

Words connect us with one another and with God. What we say and how we say it, what we write, and think all hold tremendous power. The words held in the silence of your heart are powerful too. Going deep into practices of word enables us to notice how Word really is among us.

THE STILL SMALL VOICE

And God said, Go forth, and stand upon the mount before the Lord. And behold, the Lord passed by, and a great and strong wind rent the mountains, and broke in pieces the rocks before the Lord, but the Lord was not in the wind; and after the wind an earthquake, but the Lord was not in the earthquake; and after the earthquake a fire; and after the fire a still small voice.

~ I Kings 19:11–12

Stillness reminds us of being rooted and grounded. *Smallness* reminds us of being humble and vulnerable. God's still small voice comes in silence, in spontaneous thought, in ideas that come to mind, in the whisper of a friend, or in a conversation overheard on the bus ride to work. But come when and where it may, the still small voice is heard only when we listen.

Find some space in these practices to listen for God's still small voice and use your own voice in return.

SILENCE – THE SPACE BETWEEN THE WORDS

Finding places for silence in our culture can be a challenge. It can be hard to listen for the still small voice in the midst of so much noisy activity. Our culture makes it difficult to retreat into our own silence. It encourages us to cling to the things of this world and fill all the spaces with activity. It can be a countercultural act to integrate moments of silence into your youth program.

Silence is often a new experience for people and can be the last thing they think they want. People may be afraid of what silence holds. They fear being alone in silence and what they might discover in themselves. Thinking of silence as a friend is a non-threatening way of dealing with the fear it may create.

A number of years ago, I went on an eight-day silent retreat. I had lost myself out there in the world and was facing many challenges in my personal life. I really did not know where to turn for some peace. So I signed up for the retreat.

It took me five days to slow my mind down, stop the constant thinking, and rest in God. I worked with scripture and had many dreams. I talked with a spiritual director about my own story and how it related to this time of silence. I had visions and clarity that never could have come had I not stopped all the noise in my life. I didn't want to leave. God's presence became very real and clear to me.

Perhaps you've already felt called to your own practice of silence and can tell your own story. Perhaps it's a practice you are thinking of introducing into your life. You don't have to go away for an eight-day silent retreat; space for silence can be incorporated into your life here and now. Remember that the silence we deeply need isn't the silence of the outside world but of the world inside us.

 Here are some ways to begin to introduce silence into your personal and youth ministry practices.

- *Have a one minute time of silence at the end of youth meetings. It could be a time to remember those who aren't there, pray silently, or just be still before going back out into the world. As the group becomes more comfortable with silence, extend the time. It takes time and practice to build tolerance and acceptance of silence, especially if it is a new or scary place for people.*

- *If you take your youth on an annual retreat, build silence into the retreat. Allow youth a chance to go off alone to be still and silent for an hour or so. Come back and debrief what being silent was like for them.*

- *Once your group has integrated silence into its life, you may wish to have a silent meal. Many monastic communities and retreats have community meals in silence. Start the meal with a prayer and then spend the mealtime sharing space but not voice. This practice works best for youth who have some experience with silence and feel able to take the practice seriously.*

- *Be still and know that I am God. (Psalm 46:10) Say each line of the mantra to yourself and reflect on it for a few moments.*
  Be still and know
  That I am God
  Be still
  Know that I am
  Be still
  Know
  Be still
  Be.

- *Spend the first five minutes of your day following rising in silence. Go to your window, look out on the day before you, and notice, listen, and be still. Notice what beginning the day this way feels like. No words are necessary; your prayer is simply your silence.*

- *Spend some time writing and reflecting about how silence has claimed you, or how you are waiting to be claimed by it. How do you feel about entering into silence in your life? Do you enjoy it? Is it difficult? Why are you drawn to the practice of silence? What impact do you hope it will have on your life? If you are seeking to*

be claimed by silence, plan how you will make that happen. Tell
someone about your plan and set your intention to follow through.

- *If you are serious about incorporating silence into your life,*
  make a plan to engage in a silent retreat.

GUIDED MEDITATION

This practice leads people through reflections on visual imagery using spoken word in a deeply meditative practice. This can calm, centre, and relax us. We hear God with greater clarity. The practice of relaxation in a group setting can be a tough one for youth to embrace since they are so used to movement and noise.

The practice begins with settling, then continues with the leader reading the meditation slowly, clearly, and deliberately, leaving plenty of space for people to go through their own meditation process. When the meditation is complete, have people slowly come back into the space by moving their hands and feet. People may fall asleep during the guided meditation and that is a fine response. Gently encourage them to wake up and come back to the group.

Once the whole group is back, ask people to share an image (if they saw one), or an insight that came to them. Allow people to share or keep their insights to themselves. Use the guided meditation below, or seek one out from a book or online (see resources section). I also would encourage you to create your own guided meditation.

Guided Meditation: A Gift

 Invite people to find a comfortable space (chair, floor) to settle into for this time of stillness and imagination. Once all are settled, begin. Read the following meditation clearly and slowly, leaving pauses at appropriate times during the reading.

 Welcome to this space and this time of reflection and relaxation. Take some deep breaths in and out.

Feel the air come deeply into your body. Let it go. Notice your belly rise and fall. Imagine that God is as close as your breath.

Feel your body start to relax as you focus on your breath. Let go of all tension in your body. Let yourself sink into the floor or the chair.

Keep breathing deeply and let yourself sink.

Imagine that you are walking in a place outside and there is no one else around. Perhaps you are on a beach, or in a forest, or at home in your yard. It's a good and safe place. See yourself walking through that place on your own. What do you notice about the place? How's the weather? How do you feel being in that place? Find a spot to sit and rest, and look around. Take in the space that is there for you alone.

You notice that someone in the distance is coming toward you. You begin to see who it is. How do you feel as you see this person approaching?

They get closer and you notice that they are holding something in their hand. They smile as they come closer with hand outstretched. They want to give you the thing in their hand. They are now standing before you and you reach out and take the thing they want to give you.

You look at it and look back at them. What have they given you? You pay attention to the gift, touching it, holding it.

You look up, taking in one more time where it is you are. You know that it's time to get back to your life. You get up to leave with the gift in your hand. You walk away, thinking about the gift you have been given.

Now is the time to come back to this room and this space. Slowly move your body around, rubbing your hands together, stretching your body out long, taking some deep breaths in and out. When you are ready, open your eyes, and come back to the room.

Have a five-minute break. Then invite youth to sit in a circle and share what their gift was if they wish and who the person was who came to them in their practice of meditation. Close the reflection with a prayer.

LECTIO DIVINA

Lectio Divina, or holy reading, combines speaking and silence. It is a practice of prayerful, meditative reading of scripture that has been used by the church for hundreds of years. Monastic communities began the practice as a way to bring connection with God.

The practice of *Lectio Divina* involves listening deeply to words of scripture, paying attention to the spontaneous thoughts that come as the still small voice, and then sharing your impressions. Your words may bring up insights for someone else when *Lectio Divina* is done as a communal practice. Below are two ways to engage *Lectio Divina* into a time of practicing God.

LECTIO DIVINA GROUP PRACTICE

Choose a scripture that you wish to study. Have youth sit comfortably in a circle. Light a candle to focus the practice. Explain that you will be reading the scripture through three times. Ask youth to simply listen to the first reading. Pause for a few moments.

Read the scripture again, asking youth to listen for any word or words that attract them, or raise questions for them. Following the second reading, have those who so wish share the word that they connected with.

Read the scripture for a third time, asking youth to consider how this scripture relates to their lives. Following the reading, allow youth to share how the scripture connected with their own life (if they wish to do so). Allow them to share but not comment or have conversation around what is shared. End with a time of silence and rest in the presence of God.

Lectio Divina Personal Practice

Choose a scripture that you wish to examine more deeply through the process of listening for God's voice. Find a place of quiet for yourself where you won't be distracted or interrupted. Light a candle to help you centre and remember the light of Christ is with you.

Read the passage through once, slowly and clearly, letting some words resonate and some slide away. Read the passage again, and make notes on the words that stand out and seem to be speaking to you. Say the words you have written down to yourself. Ponder them and let them sink into your being. Read the passage for the third time, noticing what the words or phrases are challenging, stirring, or comforting.

Move on to communicating with God about the things this reading has brought forth in you. You might do this silently, aloud, in writing, or through moving your body. When you have finished this active prayer, simply rest in the presence of the reading and God.

Suggested scripture readings

Mark 1:16–20	Jesus calls the fishermen
Luke 8:4–8,11–15	The good seed
Psalm 23	The Lord is my shepherd
Mark 4:35–41	Jesus calms the sea
Genesis 2:4–17	The account of creation
Luke 2:41–52	Jesus, the boy in the temple

Reading Children's Stories

Children's books are for everyone to enjoy. They tell stories in a direct and clear way, and youth relate well to them, especially those that come with beautiful images and are not too long. The ideal story to read aloud to a youth group is five to eight minutes long. I'd encourage you to visit the children's section of a library or book store, pull up a chair, and begin to explore this fantastic world. Read randomly for a while. See which stories really speak to you.

 Read a children's story at your next youth meeting. Choose a story with a positive message and follow the reading with questions about which part they liked the best and what they thought the book was trying to say. Close the story time with a prayer reflecting the theme of the book.

Another way to use children's books is to set up a story corner and allow youth to spend time there reading to themselves.

Reading the Bible Every Day

Reading scripture and knowing the stories is key to feeling more comfortable and able to share scripture with others. There are websites such as those of the American and Canadian Bible Societies that will e-mail a Bible verse to you every day. Bible studies such as the *Disciple Bible Study* cover most of the Bible in one year through intensive study and reading.

 Asking or expecting youth to read the Bible every day may be a bit much, but there may be a few individuals seeking to understand the stories in greater depth. You might create an online group that reads a Bible passage and posts reflections, thoughts, and questions each week. E-mail the passage to the group members at the beginning of each week and set a time for everyone to log on and chat about the reading together. (Some online programs provide this function free of charge.) What a cool way to combine ancient words and modern technology.

MODERN DAY WORDS OF WISDOM

Written and spoken modern day words of wisdom are everywhere in our culture: in poetry, music lyrics, stories, and newspaper and Internet articles, to name a few. In this practice we look at the words of modern poets and writers.

    Gather a collection of books of quotations, or quotes from a quote website that talk about connection with God. Print the quotes out on small pieces of paper and lay them out on a table for people to look through. Have the instructions (below) on the table also. Make sure that you give credit to the author of each quote and seek copyright permission where required.

Words of Wisdom

On the table in front of you are quotes about God from modern day poets and writers. Choose one quote that really speaks to you. Sit down with the quote and read through it a few times.

- What is the quote saying to you about your life and your connection with God?
- What drew you to this quote and what do you like about it?

You can take the quote with you and leave it somewhere where you will see it and be inspired again and again. Give thanks for the gift of the writer and poet.

You may wish to write your own words of wisdom in response to what you have read. Take a pen and paper and write your own quote or poem about God's connection in your life. Sit with what you have written and ask yourself what the quote says to you about your life and your connection with the Divine.

PRAYER GRAFFITI

This practice can be used anytime during the youth group year. It can be used as part of a spiritual practices experience, or as a practice you leave up in the youth room and allow people to contribute to over time.

 Put large sheets of paper up on a wall or provide smaller pieces of paper for people to write their prayers on and then attach to the wall. Invite people to spend some time doodling and writing their "inside" prayers in a graffiti-like manner. Then invite people to read all the prayers on the wall and say aloud the one that stands out for them. You may wish to leave the sheet(s) up in the youth room or church so others can connect with the prayers or add their own.

PRAYER POETRY

 Have a large number of unrelated words written on small pieces of paper laid out on a table. Have tape or tacks available to affix the small papers

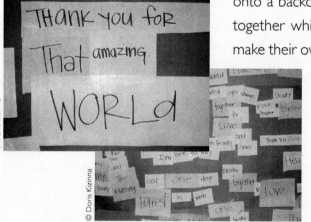

onto a backdrop on the wall. Invite youth to put together whichever words they wish on wall to make their own prayer of poetry words. They can build on prayers already created. Have a few blank pieces of paper as well in case people need a word that isn't in the pile.

You can keep this practice set up in the space or reuse the poetry prayer words on other occasions. If you wish to do that, write the words on thicker card stock paper and attach them to a bulletin board with tacks or easily removed double-sided tape. Spend some time as a group noticing the poetry prayers that have been written. Have each person choose one prayer and read it aloud at the end of your meeting.

PRAYER JOURNAL

Have youth create a prayer journal that will be used throughout the year. They could create their own books (perhaps there is a bookbinder in the congregation who could lead a workshop), or you could purchase inexpensive journals at a stationery or dollar store. Have youth decorate their journals with meaningful symbols and words. You may wish to take a photo of each youth and have them place it on the first page of their journal; then at the end of the year, take another photo for the end of the book.

Take five minutes during each meeting for youth to write down the things they are both thankful and concerned for. Remind them to date their entries. They may wish to share some of their writings. Tell youth they may use the journal when they go home as well but they must remember to bring it back to youth group the next week. Or keep the journals in a special locked box in the youth room, to be opened at each youth meeting. Recognize that for some, writing is difficult and may not be a way they can easily access their inner life. Provide another way for them to participate: a sketch book or a small hand-held tape recorder journal (available at electronic stores quite reasonably) to record in their own voice what others would write in a book. At the end of your youth group year, share in a process of looking back over your year of prayers.

POETRY NIGHT

 Invite youth to bring a poem (their own or one that someone else has written) to a group poetry night. Ask that the poem speaks to their life and their connection with God in some way. It can be serious, funny, happy, or sad. Ask them to be willing to share this poem with the group and say why the poem is meaningful. Provide a few poetry books on the night so that youth who have forgotten their poems can choose something and be included.

Recognize that there may be youth who will not feel comfortable or able to read aloud in front of a group. They might ask another person to read their poem for them, or they might participate in other ways: being the DJ for the event, or helping with the organization. Make sure you acknowledge their contribution sometime during the evening along with the others who are reading poems.

Set up the space as comfortably as possible, provide tea and snacks, and create a low-key mingling atmosphere. Have some great music playing. After people have visited for some time, call everyone together and ask people to be ready to share their poems.

Begin by reading your own poem, saying why you chose it and sharing its importance to you. Offer an opening prayer for the evening. Give thanks for the gifts of words and creativity, and for the courage of those who will be reading and sharing tonight. Put everyone's name in a hat and draw the first name. When that person is done, ask them to draw the next name out of the hat. Alternatively, have a sign-up sheet so that youth can choose in advance when to be "on."

You may wish to take a break during the evening, depending on the number of poems there are to share.

Close the evening by having everyone stand in a circle and share one line of a poem, each person building on the line spoken before them. Pass the poem prayer around by a squeeze through held hands.

WRITE A LETTER TO GOD

When was the last time you wrote a personal letter? It seems that letter writing is becoming a lost art. E-mails are quickly typed and then sent in the blink of an eye. Using paper and pen to write in your unique script, finding an envelope, going to the post office, getting a stamp, and sending your letter off is becoming a thing of the past.

There are numerous websites that give you the opportunity to write a letter to God. I found a site in Jerusalem that for a small fee will take your e-mailed prayer, print it out, and place it between the stones of the Western Wall, the last remains of God's temple. Many books have been written on this topic: *Children's Letters to God, Love Letters to God* and a whole series called *Conversations with God*. Rock star Courtney Love has written a song called *Letter to God* where she pours out her plea to God. Writing a letter to God offers us a chance to slow down and capture what we can't say out loud.

 For this practice, set up tables and chairs and provide pens, paper, and envelopes. The practice invites people to write a letter to God that expresses their longing, gratitude, and sense of connection.

A Letter to God
Take some time and write a letter to God.

Begin by closing your eyes and breathing deeply. Then take pen and paper and focus on the page before you. Allow what needs to come onto the page to come.

Be honest and open; this written letter is your prayer. Share what is in your heart, what you are thankful for, what you are longing for in your life. Let the words flow freely – don't think too much about what you are writing.

If you don't know where to start, begin with Thank you.

You are welcome to seal your letter in an envelope and take it with you. You may wish to keep it in a safe place. You may wish to mail it to yourself. You may wish to give it to someone else to read. You may wish to leave it in a special place. You may wish to throw it away. You'll know what to do with your letter.

aNONYMOUS PRaYeR

 Give each person a piece of paper and a pen and five minutes to write their own prayer. It could be a prayer of gratitude, concern, or enquiry. When everyone has finished, place the prayers into a basket or bag and have each youth draw one from the bag, suggesting that if they draw their own prayer they can either read it or put it back and draw another. Have the leader begin, then invite each person to take a turn around the circle, reading aloud the prayer that they pick. As the circle comes back to the leader, end with some closing words or a simple amen.

This practice can facilitate saying prayers aloud for youth who aren't accustomed to doing so. It can seem easier to pray on behalf of someone else.

Repeating God's Name

This practice is a meditation that uses repetitive mantra, or words that focus on the names of God. In some traditions, the repetition of God's name is done with beads or a rope with knots in it. As each bead or knot is touched, the name of God is repeated by the one who prays. In calling God's name, we are in a sense seeking God. Our calling out for the Holy One reminds us that God is here, no matter what.

Repeat the mantra below three times. You may want to create a rap with youth using the names of God. You may get youth to brainstorm a list of words they use for God and create their own prayer. This practice may be one station in a spiritual practices experience or may be chanted as a whole group.

This is a prayer to One of Many Names.
God, Creator, Spirit, Jesus.
Wise One, Holy One, Deep Mystery.
Universe Creator, Holy Spirit, Father.
Everything, Everywhere, Brother Jesus, Allah.
Ruah, Oneness, Being of Light.
Mother, Bringer of Truth, Sheltering Tree.
Breath, Music, Holy Three.
This is a prayer to the One of Many Names.
We call your name and know you are here.

CONVERSATION WITH GOD IN YOUR DREAMS

Paying attention to what we dream connects our inner and outer worlds and gives us clues about how we are connected with Deep Mystery. The Biblical tradition is full of dreams – people understood then that God speaks big time through dreams.

We all dream. Many people wake full of images from dream encounters. The practice of reflecting on and interpreting dreams is one that can be very helpful for people when seeking to resolve a situation or know themselves and God better.

Having a dream is as much a miracle as a seed germinating or the moon rising. I had a dream during a retreat that I believe was Divine communication.

In my dream, I was sitting alone in a room when a friend and colleague who I hadn't seen for some time came in. He was very changed from when I had last seen him; he was in a wheelchair and was very thin and appeared ill. I thought he must be suffering quite a lot. His face, however, was radiant. He talked to me for a long time about how he was dying and how he was so grateful for his amazing life. His radiant face and wise humble words stirred me.

He told me that he had left a gift in my room and that I should go look for it. I said goodbye, knowing that I wouldn't see him again, but feeling very blessed to have had that time with him. I then went to my room and found the walls lined with pillows that hadn't been there before, all in beautiful tones of red. Each one was unique: quilted, embroidered, rich in design and comfort, and stunningly beautiful. I was amazed that he had cared for me so much. I woke up.

I told the dream to my spiritual director the next morning, and without hesitation she pulled the following poem out of her pile of resources:

Just Sit There

Just

sit there right now.
Don't do a thing Just rest.

For your

separation from God
Is the hardest work in this world.

Let me bring you trays of food and something
that you would like to drink.

You can use my soft words
as a cushion

for your

head.

~ Hafiz

I was floored. The dream and the poem connected beautifully. I felt touched by God's presence and had a deeper understanding of what my time of retreat needed to be. It was so clearly laid out in the words of the poem and in the dream images of beautiful pillows on which to rest my head.

A nice time to introduce the topic of dreams to a group is during an overnight event. Give people an envelope and instruct them to take it with them to bed. Ask them to read what is in the envelope once they are settled into bed and ready for sleep. Inside each envelope place the following instructions.

In Your Dreams

If you are ready for sleep, spend some time looking back over the day you have just lived. Let go of the day that has been and focus on the night that is before you. Ask the Holy One to be present, keep you safe, speak to you in dreams, and show you the beautiful places that you need to see as you sleep.

Keep pen and paper beside your bed. If you have a dream in the night, wake up and jot down the points you want to remember in the morning. Next day, find a time to look over your notes and reflect on what your dreams may be saying to you.

You may wish to share the dream with your spiritual director or minister. Sometimes dreams can be disturbing, or cause intense emotions to come up. Pay attention to what you feel in light of your dreams. Talk with someone about them if you need to. Enjoy the dreams that you have and see them as a mysterious gift from yourself and God.

Prayer before sleep
Come oh God in the dreams I need this night. Come oh Spirit in dreams of comfort and security. Come oh Creator in dreams of power and call. Come Oneness in dreams of deep peace and stirring clarity. Be with me and all my brothers and sisters as we sleep. Amen.

BEST THING/WORST THING

Use the best thing/worst thing practice at the beginning of a meeting to check in on how everyone is doing. As this becomes a regular practice, youth come to rely on it as a way to share their lives and hear from one another. I used this practice quite a bit when I was in congregational youth ministry, and often it was the youth who would comment that we needed to get on to the best thing/worst thing practice. It is focused enough to hold their attention easily and doesn't offer unlimited time for sharing. It allows choice in what to share and empowers people to pray for both good and challenging situations.

This is a practice of naming the thing from the past week that you are most grateful for, along with the thing that needs some prayerful attention. Encourage everyone to participate in the circle of sharing. You might want to make notes to refer to later during prayer.

Close the practice with a leader-led prayer for the situations that people have brought to the meeting. Leave space at the end for any additional prayers. Keep the list of people's best things/worst things and during the time between youth meetings pray through the list again on their behalf.

REFLECTION

This practice is adapted from the *Ignatian Examen*, created by St. Ignatius of Loyola, the founder of the Jesuit order. It encourages self-reflection through a process of examining your actions, reactions, and presence throughout the day that has been.

    This practice can be done individually as part of a spiritual practices experience or in a group as a closing reflection on the day. If you are doing it with a group, you may wish to close the *Examen* with a group prayer, inviting participants to share their responses.

    Find a time and space where you can be still and enter deeply into this practice.

A Time to Reflect

Breathe deeply and rest in the presence of God.

Feel gratitude for the day, whatever it has been like.

Review your day from the time you awoke until this moment. Let images of the day pass through your awareness and notice how you have been in the world this day.

Notice the places in the day where you felt God near.

Notice the places in the day where you felt apart from God.

Notice the places in the day where you felt separated from other people through word or action.

Remember the places in the day that needed more wholeness and reconciliation.

Pray for strength to live a whole and reconciled life.

Give thanks for the day, whatever it was like, and pray with gratitude to be granted another day of life.

GRATITUDE

If the youth you work with are just beginning a practice of praying together, the practice of gratitude is a good place to start. You may wish to end a youth meeting with a circle of gratitude, where you as leader begin the prayer and then open up the space for people to name aloud the things they are grateful for. You may also wish to pass the prayer around the circle using an object such as a rock or a feather to focus prayer and participants. Invite people to name gratitudes or to pass the prayer if they don't wish to speak.

Another way to practice gratitude is with a meditation. Ask youth to close their eyes and mentally review their day. Read them the following meditation. Remember to read the meditation slowly and allow time for people to reflect. Do not begin the meditation until everyone is still and attentive.

At the end of the meditation ask them to name three things they are grateful for out of the day they have just lived. You may also ask them where the Holy One was present in the day.

Gratitude Meditation

 Find a comfortable place somewhere in this room. Settle in and close your eyes. Take some deep breaths in and out. Feel the air enter every part of your lungs. Feel your breath and remember that God is as close to you as your breath.

Notice things from your day that you appreciated. Hold on to those moments of gratitude. Remember how you woke up this morning. What was the first thing you saw? Remember getting ready for your day. Remember school or work. Remember the interactions you had with people. Remember what you learned. Remember where you went. Think back to what you did when you got home. Who did you talk to? What did you do? Remember coming here tonight. Remember walking in the door to this room.

Take some deep breaths in and out. Feel the air enter every part of your lungs. Feel your breath. Remember your day. Remember what you are grateful for. Remember that God is as close to you as your breath.

Slowly move your hands, your shoulders, your feet and your legs, open your eyes and come back to the room.

Following the meditation you may wish to go around the circle and have people share some of the things they are grateful for today.

FIRST THING/LAST THING PRAYER

This is a personal prayer practice for the moments after you first open your eyes in the morning and just before closing your eyes for sleep at night. It is a simple and clear acknowledgement of gratitude for what has been and what is to come.

As you open your eyes in the morning spend a few moments breathing deeply in and out, slowly waking up. From that place of comfort and rest in your bed, offer a prayer of gratitude for another day of life.

At night, just before you drift off to sleep, take some deep breaths in and out, and offer gratitude for the day that has been, thanksgiving for a night of rest, and thanks for another day of life.

BLESSING TO END THE CHAPTER

Words speak,
People speak,
God speaks,
In echoes, laughter, silence, dreams, whispers.
I lean in and I listen.
Amen.

CHAPTER 6

VISUAL ARTS AND CRAFTS

They maintain the fabric of this world,
and the practice of their craft is their prayer. ~ Sirach 38:34

Creativity is lived out in every aspect of our humanity. Many people connect most easily with the Divine Creator through their creativity. All acts of creation call us to live our best life. As you were created, so are you called to create.

For many people, recognizing, naming, and honouring a creative response in themselves is filled with self-judgment about their own ability. A common response to being asked to paint a picture or write a poem is to run screaming from the task. Those who really believe they can't draw, write, or sing, or are unused to doing so may find being asked to be creative in these ways daunting and uncomfortable. Spend some time with youth who feel this way to help them understand and move past their self-doubt. You may wish to invite an artist or art therapist to coach youth through the process of unleashing some self-expression. As always, respect where people do and don't want to go. With some direction and coaching, most youth will come to understand that creativity is something they can access. It may not be their preferred path to God, but it will at least be part of their experience of living life in all its fullness.

The following practices speak to the creative power in each individual as a response to God.

DRAWING a RESPONSE

This is a practice where youth are invited to create a free-form visual art response to a question or theme. This practice is adaptable to many different themes. I have used it to explore the concept of death and as a way to respond to the beauty of creation (as below), among other things.

This practice is intended to allow youth to share their inner selves through visual art expression.

Respect individual abilities to engage the deeper meanings of their works. Be open to group sharing following the activities, with some conversation from each person in offering their piece. You could begin the reflection with the words, "I am an artist. My prayer of gratitude for creation is…" Allow space for each person to claim the role of artist and share their reflection on their piece.

Set up a practice table with pastels, charcoal, felts, crayons, old magazines, other media, and paper and allow participants to share in the practice outlined below.

Drawing Gratitude

God's creativity is astounding.

The giraffe, the 500-year-old tree, the honey bee, all stunning.

The palm tree, the dolphin, the asparagus plant, all astounding.

The daffodil, the coffee bean, the platypus, all miracles.

Spend some time thinking of God's creation as you know it. Let images come from your heart and mind onto the paper in front of you. Use pastels, pencils or other available media.

Focus on what your prayer of gratitude for the created world is. Create!

GOD BOXES

At the beginning of each youth group year, have each youth create a God box using small cardboard boxes available from dollar stores, art shops, or the church recycling bin. Invite youth to decorate their box with colour, pictures, words, symbols, and thoughts about who they are right now and how they see God. Ask them to write some words of prayer about their hopes for the year on the bottom of the box. Throughout your year together, the box can be a place for their thoughts about God in various forms: their journal, their images, prayers and items from some of the practices. Youth may take their box home or leave it in a specially designated place in the youth room. You may ask them to bring their boxes back periodically to do more work with them, or take them along on a retreat. To end the year, you may to ask youth to unpack their God boxes and reflect on the past year together, remembering experiences and savouring all that is in their box.

PRAYER BUNDLES

This practice has youth create a small "bundle" of prayers to carry with them or place in their God box, bedroom, etc. It can be opened again and again and used in a way similar to a God box. The contents of the prayer bundle are reminders of an individual's prayer life.

 Provide for each youth either a little cloth bag or a small (30–40 centimetres) square of fabric and cord or string to tie the bundle up with. Have some supplies (see suggestions below) set out either on one large table or at several stations and invite youth to create their own prayer bundles.

Once complete, it's up to each youth to decide what they wish to do with their bundle. They may wish to take it home, leave it in the youth room (perhaps near the sacred centre), or place it in their God box. Another option is to put all the bundles together in one box and reflect on them at the end of the year.

Some suggestions for the prayer bundle

- *Print scripture verses on small pieces of paper. Youth can choose one that speaks to their life right now to roll up and place in their bundle.*
- *Have youth go outside and find a small rock to place in their bundle. Have them reflect on why they chose the rock they did.*
- *Perhaps something else from nature draws them (e.g., pine cone, twig, leaf). If it doesn't damage nature, have them place that (small!) thing in their prayer bundle.*
- *Share the story of the mustard seed (Mark 4:30–32) and give each youth a few tiny mustard seeds to place in their bundle as a reminder that mighty things can come from the smallest actions and prayers. Have some conversation about what they hope will come from the "little" prayers in their bundles.*

- *Have youth write their own prayer for their life at this time and place it in the bundle.*
- *Have youth write who or what they are praying for on a piece of paper and place it in the bundle.*
- *Include a photo of themselves or of their youth group.*
- *Invite youth to write a prayer for each person in the group and give to them to put into their prayer bundle. Suggest they not look at the prayers they have been given right away but rather find a quiet time to pray and reflect on them sometime in the next few days.*

PRAYER FLAGS

© Doris Kizinna

Prayer flags come to us from the Tibetan Buddhist culture. Traditionally, prayer flags come in five colours and have prayers and texts from the tradition written on them. Tibetans believe that prayer flags promote peace and bless the land and the people who create them. They also believe the wind catches the prayers on the flags and takes them to God.

This practice invites youth to create their own Christian prayer flags to hang in the youth room, outside the church, or take home. You will need brightly coloured fabrics cut into 35 centimetre squares. You may choose to use the symbolic colours listed below or others. Sew a three to five centimetre seam on one end of each flag (leaving ends open) so that thick string or rope can be strung through. Use fabric felts, permanent markers, or fabric paint to write prayers, messages, and images on the flags. The words and images on the flags will be a blessing to all.

You may choose to leave your flags up for the year, adding to them on occasion, or you may use them only for a special evening of practice. You may want to ask for permission to hang them outside your church building or in a garden. You may have youth put their prayer flag into their God box, or take it home and hang it up. Ideally, a prayer flag is hung where wind and Spirit can swirl around it.

Colours

Blue: Sky and space, stillness

White: Air and wind, movement

Red: Fire, passion, life force

Green: Growing things, renewal

Yellow: Land, stability

PRAYER BEADS

You may be familiar with Roman Catholic rosaries, Buddhist prayer beads, or the knotted prayer ropes from the Orthodox tradition. Prayer beads are a tangible way to aid the focus of your prayers, something to keep you "in touch" as you pray. They can also act as a reminder to put prayer into your day.

In this practice, you will create your own set of prayer beads. You may wish to wear the prayer beads on your wrist or neck and hold them in your hand when you are praying. You may wish to carry them around with you during your day, or sleep with them under your pillow. Praying with your beads may be the last thing you do before you go to sleep, or the first thing you do on waking.

 Purchase a variety of beads, along with cord or elastic to string the beads on, from a bead or craft store. You may wish to take your group members along and have them choose their own beads. The number of beads you will need will depend on bead size and the length of bracelet or necklace.

Have youth choose beads from each of the categories below so that when they use their beads their prayers will include many diverse aspects. It would be good to create a colour guide to take home, so that the meanings can be more fully integrated into the practice. You may wish to pray together using the beads.

Prayer Bead Colours

Red:

Passion, love of God, love of self, love of others. Pray for those you love and those who love you. Pray that the things you are passionate about will enter into your life fully.

Yellow:

Happiness, optimism, joy, gratitude. Give thanks for all that brings you joy and happiness, and all the blessings in your life.

© Doris Kizinna

Orange:

Creativity, wellness, openness to possibility. Ask that new possibilities enter your life. Focus on your personal health and what your body needs, and ask for it.

Green:

New life, resurrection, growth, abundance. Give thanks for your life and all you have been given. Ask that places of new growth be revealed to you.

Purple:

Oneness with God. Pray to open your heart to the presence of God. Pray for God to be revealed in your life.

Blue:

Fluidity, calmness, clarity. Breath deeply in and out and feel the calm and fluid presence of your breath. Focus on the deep breath of God in your life.

White:

Purity, your identity in truth. Ask for forgiveness for the times you haven't spoken the truth or you acted unskillfully. Ask for your heart to be pure.

Black:

Dark times in life, balance, troubled heart. Ask God to open you heart to the joy and pain of living. Offer prayers for healing the dark places in your life. Ask for balance and to learn from darkness and light.

PRAYER CLOTHS

A prayer cloth sets and beautifies a space and is a reminder to hold a space as sacred. Have each youth write or draw their prayer on it. You may wish to create one as a group for the youth room sacred space.

If doing individual cloths, have pieces of plain fabric in a variety of colours available (pieces can vary in size from a 30 centimetre square to a table-cloth size square of 120 centimetres). If working on a group cloth, have one large sized piece (tablecloth) set up so everyone can work on it together. Provide fabric pens or paints. You may wish to learn the skill of batik or tie-dying and create your group or individual cloths with this process.

Invite youth to use their imagination and creativity to design a prayer for their life or the life of the group on the cloth. Allow time and space for the process. You may wish to have meditative music playing to suggest self-reflection rather than conversation. Invite people to use their cloth in their home or office as a reminder to pray, or place it in their God box, or add to it from time to time. If you have made a group prayer cloth, find a place for it in the youth room and have the closing prayer around the cloth.

 We see our prayers on these cloths. God, you weave us together like the threads of this cloth. Holy One, who inspired these words, colours and images, be with us every time we meet to pray around this cloth. Amen.

KNITTING

Although it may seem like an old fashioned activity to introduce to youth ministry, knitting has had resurgence recently. At some of the youth events I have been involved with, knitting workshops have been surprisingly well received by the youth participants. Imagine grade nine boys walking around with knitting needles and wool and knitting in every spare moment. Wow. Talk about countercultural.

A variety of books about knitting as spiritual practice have been published in the last while (see resources section). When creative practice is linked with Spirit, the artist is connected with the Divine.

Knitting can be used as a meditation tool. Saying the same words over and over as each stitch is achieved can take us into mindfulness, where we pay attention to each stitch and allow the mind to quiet. Knitting is a tactile process that almost anyone can do. One bonus is that what you make is not only useful, but can warm and soothe. Let the knitting begin!

Invite some skilled people in your congregation to come and teach the youth group how to knit. Supply wool and needles for everyone, on the guidance of the expert knitters. Once the basic stitches have been learned, introduce a prayer practice around knitting.

Here's a sample practice you may wish to adapt:

Have people sit in a circle and begin knitting.

 Read a passage of scripture (for example, Psalm 39:13–16).

Allow some silence to be held while people keep knitting.
Invite response to the passage, encouraging people to keep knitting.
See what arises and how the conversation flows.
End with a prayer.

 Creator God, as you have knit us together, we are knitting ourselves together into a community of friendship and love. We remember a person and name them with each stitch. (Hold some space for people to knit for a minute or so, and have them name the names of those who they are remembering either silently or aloud.) *Be with us here, in the practice of this craft, in the creation of beauty, in connection with one another. We pray.*
Amen.

 You may also wish to do a *Lectio Divina* practice while knitting (see page 114). Read the scripture three times and seek a response after each reading.

PRAYeR SHaWLS

Prayer shawls have been used in various traditions for centuries as a way to provide comfort and warmth to others, as ritual clothing for religious ceremony; and as a reminder of God's loving embrace. They can be given to those in need of comfort, support and care, or to mark a special occasion such as welcoming a baby.

 As with all practices, intention makes the difference. Begin by imaging who it is you are making the shawl for, then hold that person in mind and offer prayers as you work. When the prayer shawl is complete, a final blessing is said on behalf on the person receiving it. Also say a prayer of gratitude for those who have helped in its creation.

Knitting a shawl can be a long process, especially if people are not expert knitters, but shawls can also be made from cozy fabric. Cut pieces that wrap nicely around a person and decorate with beads, charms, fringe, other pieces of fabric, patches, or words that highlight the intention of providing comfort and care. You may wish to enlist the help of an expert sewer for this practice.

 Loving enfolding God, bless our hands as we create a shawl of strength, comfort, faith, and care. Bless our work so that the one receiving this shawl will receive all that they need. May they know they are not alone. Your loving presence is around them as this shawl is around them. Protect them and strengthen them. We pray.
Amen.

QUILTING

Making a quilt with a group of people can be a satisfying experience. Quilting groups all over the world work passionately to create beauty, form, and function from scraps of fabric.

Invite people in your congregation to donate fabric they no longer have a use for. You may also wish to go to a quilt store and purchase fabric, if budget allows.

Once you have all the fabric, plan an evening or day-long quilt-making workshop. Ideally, invite a quilter or two from your congregation (there will be some, guaranteed), or someone from a local quilt shop to come and give a workshop on how to piece together a quilt. If you feel confident in leading on your own, a great place to start is to have each youth contribute a square or piece.

As a group, you may wish to make one quilt for the youth room, or to give away as a gift. You may wish to make more than one quilt, or make small quilts to give away to babies in the congregation or as a mis-

© Doris Kizinna

sion project. Start with one quilt and see how it goes; this may be a practice that you and your youth are drawn to and one that you'd like to continue as regular practice and ministry. You may wish to keep your quilt in your youth room to be used when people need a nap, comfort, or just want to be wrapped in the beauty and creativity of the group.

The quilt on the left is one that I created using symbols of things that were important to me at that time. Inviting youth to make a symbol quilt is one idea for a group project.

A suggested scripture to use in conjunction with quilting is I Corinthians 12:4–11.

 God has created us individual and unique, just as the squares in this quilt are individual and unique. Each one different, each one of the same Spirit. We give thanks for the wonder in diversity – so many differences, so much to know about one another. May this quilt be stitched with love, and may we know how connected we are to our friends in this circle and the body of God, who is like a warm soothing quilt of diversity.
Amen.

COLLaGe

Collage is a form of visual art that incorporates diverse elements. The collage project I introduce here is a two-dimensional art piece on paper created in response to questions and prayer.

When introducing this practice of collage, begin with a prayer and the directions (see suggestions below). Encourage people to allow the creative process just to happen. Collage is about experimenting. Randomly place items on a page and see how they look. Shift and move pieces around as desired. Encourage people to work with a theme or message they want to share, using images and words to bring that message to life.

In preparation for this practice, gather magazines, pictures, colour copies of pictures, old calendars, newspapers, old flyers, or anything else that you would like to use for two-dimensional collage. Gather scissors, glue sticks, watercolour or acrylic paints and brushes, and cardboard, card stock, or art paper for backing material.

The following process can be done in a group setting. Begin with the reading below and direct people through the process of creation, reflection, and sharing. This practice encourages people to share who they are with one another. Either ask youth to share individually when done or come together in a circle and ask each person to share with the group.

You may wish to create a collage exhibit at your church or in your youth room and invite others to come and get to know the youth group through their work.

 The pieces laid out on the table are all pieces of possibility awaiting your hand to bring them together.

Close your eyes and focus on your prayer. When you feel calm and connected to the many pieces of who you are, begin choosing pieces for your prayer collage. Without thinking about it all too hard, let the pieces of your being come to life on the page before you. Choose, cut, rip, draw, use colour, glue, layer, and create.

When you feel finished, set your piece aside and spend some minutes away from it. Clean up the space, connect with others for a while. Then go back to your collage and focus on it for some time. What thoughts come to you? What prayers do you see? What words can you put to the piece you have created? What major themes have come out in the collage?

PHOTOGRAPHY

There may be individuals in your youth group who are keen on photography and on creating slide or PowerPoint presentations. In this practice, youth work together with a prayer theme. They photograph images relevant to the theme and then put together images and words in a presentation. It can be used for youth group or with the whole congregation.

The practice of stopping, being still, noticing, focusing on one thing, and capturing the image can be a meaningful experience for the one taking the pictures. The end result can open something unexpected in those viewing the photos.

 Choose a theme together and work on the project individually or in small groups. In my experience, youth can become very excited and engaged in this kind of practice. It not only helps them slow down, but builds community and generates conversation on themes that wouldn't ordinarily come up. The finished photography prayer could be accompanied by words (projected with the slides), used as a visual backdrop for spontaneous prayer spoken in response to the pictures, or projected with music.

Possible themes
- Creation and the earth
- Small things
- People
- Understanding
- Issues that teens face
- The presence of Jesus in the modern world

FILM MAKING

Creating a short film on a faith theme can be a lovely way to engage youth in using technology to put their message "out there." Their short film will undoubtedly be up on YouTube within hours of creation and can then be accessed by people around the world. Almost every digital camera comes with the ability to take video clips. Some youth will also have the software to edit those clips with.

As with the photography practice, it is important to spend some time as a group discovering the message you'd like to create. Creating script and process guidelines in advance of filming helps alleviate chaos during the filming. I will again say that it is important to have some idea of where you are going as a group before you start shooting the film.

 The group may decide to have people share their thoughts interview-style, or they may wish to enact a story (ancient or modern). They may wish to incorporate images and music related to their theme. Work with editors to bring to life the message of prayer and spiritual practice that the group wants to share. I would recommend keeping it simple. Simple and beautiful images are often the most effective in film making.

When the film is complete, arrange a time for others from the community to come and watch. Perhaps have a screening following worship on Sunday morning or during one of the services. This way the prayer reaches the lives of others.

DRAWING ICONS

Creating personal icons can be a way to bring a story to life. Show youth images of icons from around the world. You may use a book of icons (see resources section) or create your own PowerPoint slide show using free online images. Also see the praying with icons section (page 90) for more inspiration on working with icons.

 Have youth choose a story or person from scripture that stands out for them and then allow time for them to make their own personal icon about that story or person. You may also choose one story and read it with the group, sharing in a *Lectio Divina* practice with the scripture. Then invite each youth to create an icon on that story. It will be interesting to see how different icons are created from the same story. Provide paint, pastels, pencil crayons, and good quality thick art paper. You may also wish to provide images from magazines or other sources that will help those who don't feel able to paint or draw solely from their imagination.

Have youth share their finished icons by talking about the person or story that prompted them to create their piece and why they felt drawn to it. You may wish to ask them to tell the story from memory so that it really sinks in. You may wish to create an icon gallery for the congregation, so that others can be inspired by the messages of the stories.

© Jes Beckerley

INDIVIDUAL MANDALA

The mandala circle has been used in many religious traditions. Ancient Christian mystics, First Nations (medicine wheel), Aztecs, Taoists (yin and yang), and Tibetans, among others, have used the circle and spiral to signify their inner spiritual journey and longing for wholeness.

Provide youth with a template of a circle on a large piece of paper or invite them to create their own on provided paper. Provide a variety of visual art supplies: pastels, paints, crayons, pencil crayons, pens, and inks. Share an opening prayer and the instructions. Have some books on classical and modern mandalas available (see resource section) so people can explore the concept.

Making a Mandala

This is the practice of the circle of wholeness that is your life. You are going to create a mandala, which is a circle that tells a story. Something from your life is speaking to you today. This is a way to share your mandala story.

Spend some time looking at the four story categories below and begin to draw pieces of your story from each category inside, outside, or all around the circle. Whatever you create or share is just the right thing. Alternatively, do the same thing with the prayer categories or combine prayers and stories.

Spend some time creating and then we'll share our stories through sharing our mandalas.

Mandala Story Categories

- Tell us about your life as a child.
- Tell us about the best and the worst times in your life.
- Tell us what your life is full of right now.
- Tell us some of the lessons you've learned so far in life.

Mandala Prayer Categories

What are the prayers that are in your heart today for

- Yourself
- Others
- The world
- God

GROUP MANDALA

Work together without speaking to create a piece of group artwork. Each person may use one specific area of the mandala space, or the group may choose a freeform style where work is intermingled and plays off what is there. Whatever is created will be a thing of beauty; it may even amaze you!

You will need a large space and a large circle cut from heavy paper. You may need to tape pieces of paper together to form a large sheet and then cut a circle out of that. Provide visual art supplies: pastels, paints, crayons, pencil crayons, pens, inks, brushes, magazines, newspapers, etc.

Begin the group mandala practice with the meditation below and then invite people into a time of deliberate creation. Ask people to work in silence. Provide some soft background music. Allow people space to create until they feel finished. Once the mandala is done, ask youth to stand

and move around it and notice what has been created. Stand and move in silence.

Close with the following prayer:

Creating God, together we created this work of art. We are a community and have unique gifts to bring to one another. We thank you that as you created so we create. We pray for one another and as we look around this circle at one another, we offer silent prayers of gratitude and blessing for wholeness and peace. (Hold space for silent reflection.)

Pass the peace of Christ to one another. (See page 233.)

GROUP MANDALA MEDITATION

Have youth sit comfortably in a circle. Close eyes, take some deep breaths together – three breaths, inhaling and exhaling together (leader count). Speak slowly and allow pauses where appropriate.

- *Imagine that there is a place high above you, beyond the clouds, where the light is bright, golden, warm.*
- *Imagine the light from high above you pouring down on you and the group. The light surrounds everyone and gets in everywhere.*
- *Feel the light moving, warm, protective, and loving. Feel how the light connects with everyone in the group. Sense the light loving everyone.*
- *As you continue to breathe, feel each breath drawing down more warm loving light. It surrounds you and fills your heart even more.*
- *Imagine the light gathering in a round pool at the centre of your circle.*

- *Bring to mind your deepest prayer and from your heart let it flow into the pool of light in the centre of the circle. Notice how the colours and light move and change. Notice the words that may form on the surface of the pool. The prayers of everyone in the circle are being created before your very eyes.*
- *Keep breathing. Notice the loving energy, the colours and images, imagining together a prayer.*
- *When you are ready, open your eyes and as a group, create a mandala that brings to life the prayer you saw in the circle of light.*

SCRAPBOOKING

Scrapbooking has become widespread in North America as a favourite pastime that keeps treasured memories alive. You may have people in your program who are already into scrapbooking.

 This spiritual practice asks youth to create a prayer scrapbook of those people, situations, and places that they would like to hold in prayer. Youth may create a page for an important person in their lives and include a photograph and some words about what that person means to them and what they might pray for them about. Youth may wish to pray for certain situations in the world and incorporate photographs or newspaper headlines about those situations. They may wish to create a page about a conflict or situation in their own life that is calling out for reconciliation.

You can use a bound journal for this practice or bind individual pages into a book or binder yourself. There are many items available from scrapbooking or dollar stores that can be used to decorate the pages.

Create this book intentionally and prayerfully. Spend some time thinking about who to include. Use the book during times of prayer. Let the book fall open to a page and use that as your prayer focus, or leaf through the book and pray a short word for each person/situation. Add notes and comments as things change.

The prayer scrapbook is something that can be kept, treasured, and used throughout your life. What an amazing treasure – a book of your prayers from the time you were a teenager. Many youth will enjoy this practice of focused creativity. Enter now into the scrapbooking world!

PRAYER TO END THE CHAPTER

Spirit of Life, Great Creator. Hands open to create, to receive.
Thought, dream and word come to life in colour, light and form.
Divine Life, Inspired Creator, grant us eyes to see, hands to create,
inspired hearts open to Life and Presence, creating always. Amen.

CHAPTER 7

BODY aND MOVEMENT

*Your body is a temple
of the Holy Spirit within you.* ~ I Corinthians 6:19

Practices of movement engage our wonderfully made parts in praising God. Earthy and sacred, whole and fragile, scarred and miraculous, our body is the house in which God lives and our way to be in the world. We are divine, yet we easily forget how divine we really are.

Christianity evolved in a way that emphasized head-centred practices of word and thought. The place where all parts of the body engage in divine practice was left behind. Typical Sunday morning worship services in mainline denominations include very little time to allow body response to Spirit. It might thus be said that less is expected or asked of those worshipping – it's easy just to sit back and let someone else do the moving. Some churches understand the value of body involvement and response and include standing, taking on prayer postures, raising hands, and dancing in their services of worship. These practices ask those gathered to participate rather than simply receive. They call us to show up fully alive and present to God.

This chapter contains practices that involve the whole body in prayer and worship. If this is brand new territory for you, I'd encourage you to try it. Movement as a spiritual practice is a way to bring all of your wonderfully made parts to Holy Presence.

BReaTH PRacTICeS

Breathing is the single most important thing we do. Without it, we do not live. Usually we pay little attention to it – it just seems to happen.

Breath practices recognize the breath's fundamental nature and connection with the Source of Life. Even a practice as simple as noticing a breath connects us to God. Breathe in, and welcome the Holy into our life; breathe out and let go of what we no longer need. God's presence can be described as being as close as the breath within us, and just as essential and life-giving.

Pay attention to how you feel when you are conscious of your breathing and how sustained deep breathing calms and nourishes you. Images and thoughts may come to you during the following practices. Pay attention to what you notice. Paying attention to breath is prayer and meditation. The breath is the stuff of the Divine; each response is a pull to life in all its fullness.

Are you looking for me? I am in the next seat.

My shoulder is against yours.
When you really look for me, you will find me

instantly –
You will find me in the tiniest house of time.

Kabir says: Student, tell me, what is God?
He is the breath inside the breath.

~ Kabir

Breath Practice 1: Breathe Deeply

Sit comfortably and be still. Close your eyes. Breathe into the deepest part of your belly. Let your belly rise with each inhalation and fall with each exhalation. Allow your breath to slow. Breathe slowly and deeply. Focus just on your breath. If thoughts come into your head, notice them and let them go. Come back to the feeling of the breath coming into your body. Notice the feeling of it coming in and then notice how it feels leaving your body.

When you are complete with this practice, be conscious of the gratitude you may feel for the gift of breath. Be conscious of how your body feels after being nurtured through breath.

Breath Practice 2: Breathing in *Yah-weh*

Speaking the word *Yahweh*, (yah-way) Hebrew for God, is practically effortless. *Yah-weh*, two simple syllables.

Sit quietly and comfortably, close your eyes, and focus on your breathing. Breathe deeply and slowly into your belly, filling your body with breath. Long and deep, in and out. Let any thoughts roll away. Focus on the breath.

Breathe in and say the word *yah* to yourself within your breath. Breathe out and say the word *weh* within your breath. Breathe in *yah*, the very name of God. Breathe out *weh*. Breathe in *yah* again. Breathe out *weh*. Repeat. Continue on with calling God's name through your breath for as long as you wish. Notice what images or words come to you.

Breath Practice 3: Slowing Down the Breath

This practice slows down breathing and relaxes the body. Breathe deeply in and out for about one minute. Focus on how the breath enters and leaves your body. Then inhale while counting to four. Hold the breath for four counts, then release the breath while counting to four. Pause for a count of four, then inhale again for four counts, hold for four, exhale for four, pause for four. Continue with this cycle of four count for as long as you wish. You may also wish to extend the count to five, six, or seven. Breathing in this way slows the breath, clears the mind, and produces a feeling of relaxation. Use it as a way to calm and clear your mind in preparation for other practices.

Breath Practice 4: Yearning and God's Name

This prayer helps us remember who God is to us and offers a prayer for what we need in our lives. Choose a word you would use for God (God, *Ruah*, Life, Spirit, Holy One, One, Being, Jesus, Almighty) and as you breath in say that name either within yourself or aloud. Choose another word that expresses a longing you have for yourself (peace, love, joy, wholeness, healing). As you breathe out, say the word that expresses your longing. Breathe in the name you would give God. Breathe out what you are yearning for. Repeat this breath prayer over and over.

I breathe in Divine Spark. I breathe out calm. I breathe in Divine Spark. I breathe out calm.

Continue until you feel yourself entering into the prayer and the breath, calling on God. Stop when it feels right. Notice if you feel different than when you first started.

BREATH MEDITATION

Invite people to get comfortable, either sitting or lying down. Share the following meditation. Speak slowly and leave pauses between phrases so people can focus and imagine.

Get comfortable. Get a bit more comfortable.

Close your eyes.

Begin to notice your breath.

Notice your breath as it moves in through your nostrils and out through your mouth.

Now as you take a long, slow, deep breath in, follow the path of that breath as it moves through your nasal passages, into your throat, and into your lungs.

Feel its coolness.

Notice any fragrance it carries.

Notice any sound it makes as it is drawn into your body.

Notice any irritations or delights it offers you.

As you breathe out, notice the way your body responds.

How is it for you as you receive breath?

How is it for you as you return breath?

Follow your breath for a few moments. Don't control it, simply rest in the rhythm of your own breath.

After breathing this way for some time, give thanks for the gift of life, the gift of breath.

When you are ready, slowly begin to move your arms and legs, stretch yourself out and open your eyes and come back to this place and these people around you.

MOVEMENT PRACTICE

 This practice can be used as a group practice or as a station at a spiritual practices experience. If using as a station, have the instructions laid out for people to refer to. If using in a group practice lead people through the practice verbally.

 Take off your shoes and/or socks if you wish.

Stand with your feet firmly grounded. Notice your connection to the earth.

Hold your hands in prayer position in front of your heart. Breathe deeply into this position.

Raise your hands above your head, palms facing outward, reaching to the heavens. Breathe deeply into this position.

Bring your hands down to your sides, breathing deeply into the position.

Repeat the cycle as many times as you wish: prayer position, heavenward position, and arms at sides position, breathing deeply into each position.

Notice how the body feels in each pose.

Breathe in and savour your body movements.

End the practice with a prayer of gratitude for your ability to move your body, however that is, and for the freedom you feel in movement.

PRAYER POSES

Most faiths have a traditional way of holding the body in prayer. It may be kneeling; moving from standing to kneeling to prostrating; sitting quietly with head bowed, hands clasped, and eyes closed; or sitting cross-legged. Kneeling in prayer is an expression of full body prayer as well as a humbling act of homage.

Moving your body into a new prayer pose can bring insight about your practice and your relationship with the Holy. Think about the pose you generally take when you are in prayer. What is your faith's general way of praying? Do you feel connected to God in this pose? Have you tried any other postures of prayer?

The following practice allows people to experience a variety of prayer postures. You may wish to use this as a station in a spiritual practices experience or lead a group through it.

 In preparation for this practice put a blanket or carpet on the floor for people to practice on. Have a kneeler available. Read the following outline or have it written out for people to follow.

The Body Prays

With my hands I praise God; with my feet, my legs, my heart, my head, my fingers, my toes, my mouth I praise God. I show up with my whole body alive to God's presence, with my whole body praising God. You who gave me life, who gave me breath, who created my heartbeat, I praise you with all of my beautiful parts.

At this practice station spend some time in different prayer positions. Offer a heartfelt prayer in each posture. You may wish to offer the same prayer in all the postures you explore. Notice which postures feel right. Notice which are uncomfortable. Notice which push you to a more alive place. It may not be physically possible for you to do some of the postures suggested here. Do whichever ones you can.

Here are some possibilities.

- kneeling (use the kneeler provided)
- kneeling with knees on the earth, arms raised
- standing with your hands in prayer pose (hands touching in front of your heart centre)
- standing with your hands raised above your head
- kneeling with head on the floor, arms resting on the floor at your sides (baby pose)
- lying face up with your arms at your sides
- lying face down with your arms your sides
- sitting cross-legged on the floor with hands resting on your knees
- sitting in a chair with your hands in prayer pose
- standing on your head (if possible)

Hold each prayer pose for as long as you wish. After you have completed as many as you wish, repeat the pose you felt most drawn to. End the practice with thanks for your body's ability to move and explore news ways to pray.

HeaLING TOUCH

Many denominations have begun to integrate the ministry of healing touch into their mission and work. Healing touch is a practice of working with energy to comfort, soothe, relax, and heal the body and soul. You may have a healing touch group or practitioner in your congregation. You may wish to further the practice of healing touch in your own youth ministry and have a person come in and hold a practice session or workshop on healing touch with the youth. It is a prayerful practice of centring and compassion that youth relate well to.

 The following is a way to practice healing touch on yourself that can be done anywhere. It is a practice that can be self-directed and used as a station in a spiritual practices experience, or one person could lead a group through it.

 Sit comfortably in a chair or lie down on the floor. Breathe deeply as you settle into your position. As you hold your hand on the various parts of your body, focus on blessing, soothing, and generating compassion for yourself.

Place your hand over your heart and hold it there for a few minutes, noticing the energy and heat generated between your heart and your hand. This place is the centre of your being, your love and compassion. Give thanks for the love you receive and the love that you give.

Move your hand to your forehead or the top of your head and hold it there for a few minutes, feeling the energy there. This is the place of insight, thought, and connection with the Divine. Give thanks for the presence of God.

Move your hand to your solar plexus, just above your navel and rest it there for a few moments. Feel the energy of your centre. This is the place of action and movement, the core of who you are. Give thanks for the gift of your being in the world.

End with your hand on your heart again. Feel the warmth generated. Ask God to bring healing, warmth, and wholeness to your being. Ponder what blessing you most need on this day. Offer that to your-self in the form of a prayer, and offer a prayer of gratitude for the gift of touch.

DANCE CHURCH

Imagine a softly lit room and techno dance beats sounding from speakers. Imagine a group of people of all ages moving to the rhythm, dancing however they wish, filling the space with energy. Imagine the DJ is the church music director, the dance leader is the minister, the music is the sermon, the dancers are the congregation. Dance church! An experience that offers you a chance to sweat your prayers and allow Spirit to enter into body and heart through movement. It's been called ecstatic or trance dance, and is variously practiced in many traditions. We imagine Sufis in their white robes whirling themselves into ecstatic prayer; we look to Aboriginal traditional dance; and we think of youth finding a place to belong and simply be in the beat of a rave. We understand that dance in the realm of Spirit is a spontaneous response where the body moves as the body will to bring release, vitality, and wholeness. Dance church is a place for people to discover and amplify their Holy connection through dance, free of judgment, instruction, or the confines of a "right way to do it."

Instead of holding the usual youth dance, hold dance church instead. A dance leader or DJ may introduce the concept of movement as prayer and give participants a chance to focus on that. They may wish to lead people into a circle dance to connect and build community. You may have a portable labyrinth that you could set up in the space and offer other spiritual practices set up around the space for folks who need a rest from dancing. Dance church may go on for an hour or two; longer if you wish.

However you do it, dance church can become a vital and full body practice for your youth program.

JOY BaLLOONS

 Bring a large sealed box full of blown up balloons into the space where youth are meeting. Have an envelope containing the scripture (Psalm 16:11) and the prayer below taped to the top of the box. Place the box in the middle of the room and sit nearby, building anticipation for the youth about what is in the box. Open the envelope and take out the paper. Hopefully by this time you will have everyone's attention. If not, gather them in.

Read aloud the scripture and prayer and then crazily rip open the box of balloons. Pull them out and throw them around. Play the game of keeping the balloon in the air. Play and celebrate God's presence in the fun of the game, the beauty of the colours of the balloons, the joy of being together.

When things wind down, ask youth to form a circle and hold a balloon. Hand out markers and ask each person to write with the marker on the balloon the things that bring them joy. Play the balloon toss game again for one more minute and have each person end up with another person's balloon. As a closing prayer, have them read aloud things that bring another person joy. This is a practice of sharing simple joy, the best kind.

I awake with a remembering of joy. It lives somewhere deep down, undiminished. Perhaps somewhere in the silent night of my heart deep joy rumbles. It's waiting for us to remember. Amen.

I BOW DOWN

Share this movement practice as an opening or closing of a youth meeting. Repeat it three times. The first time through, leader reads words line by line, with actions, and group members repeat words and follow actions. Second time through, say it and do the actions together. Third time, just do the actions with no words.

I bow in the presence of God. (Hands together in prayer pose in front of heart. Bow.)

I receive the love and grace of God. (Lift hands up above head, palms open, receiving.)

I bow in the presence of all those with whom I share my life on earth. (Hands together in front of heart in prayer pose. Bow.)

I seek to understand the struggles others go through. (Hands outstretched in front of body, a gesture of giving.)

I bow into my own awakened heart. (Hands together in front of heart. Bow.)

Cherishing, loving and caring for myself. (Hands crossed over heart.)

I bow and give thanks for all those who have prayed here today. (Hands together in prayer pose in front of heart. Bow.)

PRACTICES OF PILGRIMAGE

A Great Pilgrimage

> *I felt in need of a great pilgrimage*
> *so I sat still for three*
> *days*
> *and God came*
> *to me.*

~ Kabir

Pilgrimage Practice 1: Wilderness Practice

Opportunities for most youth to be alone in nature are rare. This practice fits well into a retreat or a day long practices experience and serves as a way to reflect on the experience. For example, spend the morning experiencing various practices and after lunch invite youth to undertake their own wilderness practice. You may have a large park close by with areas to explore, or you may be meeting at a camp or retreat centre with a lot of outdoor space.

 Send youth out with a water bottle and their journal for some time (at least 30 minutes) on their own in silence in nature. Remind youth to notice what they hear, smell, see, and feel. Ask them to enter into the space and pray in their own way. Ask them to refrain from interacting with one another during the time of the practice. Remind them that the purpose is to simply be in the natural world noticing and experiencing. Invite them to spend time sitting, walking slowly, paying attention to the sounds, smells, and images that are around them. Invite them to notice what thoughts come to them. For many youth this may be a very tough challenge; encourage them to try. Be sure that people are within sight of one another so that no one gets lost. Clearly define the boundaries of where youth need to stay and have a leader remain at a central location. Youth may check in with the leader if necessary. If they do, they should be encouraged to go back and stay with the process.

When the time is up, call youth back with a bell or gong. Find a quiet place and sit together in silence for five minutes, then open a time of sharing with a prayer of thanksgiving. Ask youth to share what they noticed. What did they hear, see, smell, and feel? What was their experience like?

After everyone has shared, spend time in a closing prayer of thanksgiving for creation and for silence.

Pilgrimage Practice 2: Prayer in the Rock

The Western or Wailing Wall in Jerusalem is a remnant of the Holy Temple that stood during Jesus' time. People travel to Jerusalem to leave prayers in the clefts and cracks of the wall.

 The following practice is similar to the one that people undertake at the Wailing Wall. I invite you to take your group to a place outdoors such as a beach, a mountain top, the church garden, or a park near you. The outdoor world is sacred space regardless of where it is.

Recount stories of people going on retreat to pray and reflect on their lives, and how Jesus went into the wilderness to do this. Share how this practice incorporates the story of the Wailing Wall. Share also that this is a symbolic act that we do to remember our prayers and our connection with God. God won't magically come and read our prayers but God within us already knows our prayers and concerns.

Give each person pen and paper and ask them to find a spot in the wilderness place (not straying too far from the group) and write their own prayer. Invite them to write about what is on their hearts. Instruct them to leave their prayer somewhere out in the wilderness, perhaps in the cleft of a rock or in the crook of a tree. Doing so connects them to their ancient faith and is a reminder that there are many ways to pray to God.

Call youth back with the bell or gong and share some closing words on going back into the world after this experience.

Pilgrimage Practice 3: Labyrinth

There has been resurgence of the use of ancient and traditional faith practices as we expand and elevate our search for connection to the Divine. We search for wisdom and understanding today through what has worked for people in the past.

The practice of walking a labyrinth is an ancient practice of prayer, pilgrimage, and meditation whose roots go back thousands of years. In Christianity, the labyrinth played a vital part in the practice of pilgrimage. When an actual journey to a sacred site was not possible, people walked the labyrinth. Labyrinths were present on the floors of some of the Christian faith's oldest and most beautiful cathedrals. Although the practice of walking the labyrinth fell into disuse for centuries, it is again becoming a powerful Christian practice as people search for wisdom in the old traditions.

 If your church does not have its own labyrinth, there may be one in your community that you aren't aware of. Ask around or check online. You may wish to create your own labyrinth to use with your group and your church. There are many kinds of labyrinths – research options that might work for you. You can make an easily moved and stored labyrinth on canvas or paint a more permanent one on a gym floor. Create one outdoors with stone, gravel or grass, or have fun with a temporary labyrinth on the beach.

Consider the labyrinth a tool of meditation and prayer. The path takes us to the centre of a circle and then, after a pause, sends us back out into the world. The practices are varied: for some it's a chance to walk slowly, meditatively, breathing deeply into each step; for others it's a dance to

© Doris Kizinna

the centre. Sometimes a question will arise as you are walking to the centre; in the centre perhaps an answer will come. I have walked the labyrinth many times and each time I experienced it differently. Sometimes I walked slowly, sometimes I sang, sometimes I prayed aloud, sometimes I was stopped in my tracks by an image in nature that I hadn't noticed before. Sometimes I felt nothing but my steps, sometimes my questions were answered, and sometimes I saw visions. It's always a mysterious walk and it is a beautiful way to practice prayer.

Youth are particularly drawn to the practice of walking the labyrinth. It is about prayer-full movement and action; it is mysterious and ancient and special. People sense something holy about the labyrinth that is not easily expressed. I encourage you to enter into the practice of the labyrinth in your youth ministry program. Find a labyrinth, build a labyrinth, use a labyrinth, walk a labyrinth, ask questions about the labyrinth, research the labyrinth, and when done praying in it, reflect on it together. (See resources section.)

Pilgrimage Practice 4: Mindful Walking

This practice of pilgrimage is simply walking as prayer.

Each time our feet touch the earth, they send a prayer. Walking intentionally grounds us in the awareness of how we belong to the natural world. It is amazing, given the size of our bodies, that it is usually only the soles of our feet that touch the earth. We meet God's earthy sacredness through our feet.

For most people, walking is an everyday activity that is easy to take for granted. People who are unable to walk can practice mindful walking in other ways, such as moving in a wheelchair or by visualizing walking in their mind. They may have some insights to offer the group about what it is like to touch the earth in other ways than with their feet. Talk with them about how this practice can be adapted for their life.

 I've listed below some ways to introduce the spiritual practice of mindful walking into your program. As with all practices, it is the intention that you bring to the act that transforms it into a spiritual practice.

- *Take a walk with your group around the place where you meet. Pray together that eyes will see God's presence during the walk. Encourage people to walk slowly and pay attention to what they are noticing. Come back to where you started the walk and have each person share where they noticed God's presence in their walk. End the walk with a short prayer of gratitude for the company of walkers and God's presence.*
- *You may wish to have a massage therapist or a reflexologist come to your youth meeting to talk about foot care and demonstrate simple exercises that people can do for themselves or for one another. The evening could involve a foot washing practice and then a time of having each person's feet cared for with massage.*

Feet are a tender issue for many people. Trusting others in the group will be the key to making this practice enjoyable for youth. End the time or practice with a prayer of gratitude for the gifts of touch, compassion, and relaxation. Yeah feet!

- *You may wish to participate in a walk for a cause in your community. The trick again is to set the intention to walk in a way that connects you with each another, the cause you are walking for, the earth, and God. Remind people to allow each step to be a prayer. Perhaps count or say a word with each step to help with focusing. Notice how your feet touch the earth and how it feels to walk mindfully for a cause.*

Pilgrimage Practice 5: Pilgrimage around Your Church

This practice is a journey of sorts, a pilgrimage in your own church building. The people in the group (youth and leaders) encounter one another, the building, and God in a practice of walking, exploring, and reflecting together.

You will walk in silence from room to room, reflecting on the life of the church, then gather at certain spots to light a candle and say a prayer. The leader will pose a question and invite response. Following the pilgrimage, you will gather for a feast that the leader has brought. You can adapt this practice so that it works with your group and building, as well as the level of community development and storytelling you are seeking.

Church Pilgrimage Practice

Have with you a backpack containing four votive candles (in small holders that can carry lit candles safely), matches, enough cookies for everyone in the group, and supplies for the feast after the pilgrimage (bread, cheese, grapes, or other symbolic food). Gather people at the main entrance of the church, take one of the candles from your backpack and light it. Give it to one of the youth to hold, and read the following prayer:

Welcoming God, we are standing at your door and knocking. We have gathered together in your name and we wait to welcome one another and begin this walk in your presence. Holy One, we give thanks for all those who have entered these doors and served, making this a place of community, friendship, and faith. Welcoming God, we are here. Grant us peace as we walk this path tonight. Help us open to your presence and understand one another. As we are welcomed, so we welcome others.
Amen.

Invite people to share in a welcome together. Pass the peace with a handshake, a hug, a smile, and say to each other, "Welcome to this place."

Once all have shared in the welcome, enter the building and process silently with the lit candle to the kitchen. Once there, take another candle from your backpack, light it, and pass it to another youth to carry. Pull out some cookies from your backpack, enough for one for each person, and place them on a plate.

Read the following prayer:

God, you make a home for us in this place. Here is a warm kitchen for us to be in. Candlelight. A circle of friends. A plate of cookies. God we give thanks for the life of service that so many people live out in this place.
Amen.

Pass around the cookies. Ask youth, "How has this church been like a home for you? If it hasn't been like a home, what could you imagine would make it more like a home for you?" Allow time for sharing around the circle. Once the sharing is complete, process in silence to the darkest place in the church (basement room, boiler room), taking with you the first two candles, still lit.

Light the third candle from your bag and allow people to settle into the space. Have only the light of the candles if possible. Allow people to sink into the silence.

After some moments of silence, share in this prayer:

Oh God of the dark and of the light. We know life is full of beautiful, fulfilling, meaningful moments when life makes sense. We know that life is full of overwhelming, desperate, lost moments when nothing makes sense. We know that there are times too where we simply exist in neither joy nor sorrow. Whether we live in the light or the dark or the grey, we know deep down that Mysterious Presence loves us in all our ways of being. God be with us tonight in this dark, quiet place and let us sit and share some of our own stories.
Amen.

Invite people to share how they see their lives at this time. Are they in the light, are they in the dark, are they in the grey? What is their prayer for the space they are in?

When all who wish to have shared, gather the candles and people together and walk in silence to the final stop on the pilgrimage, the front of the sanctuary.

Take out of your backpack another candle, light it, and place it with the other three. Take out the feast of bread, grapes, cheese, or other symbolic snack.

Pray together.

Oh God of belonging. This is a place of belonging. It belongs to us and we belong to it. It connects us to you and to Jesus. Because we came into these doors on this night, because we shared cookies and a place called home, because we shared our light and dark, because we gave thanks and walked together, we belong here. Nothing can ever separate us from your love, no matter where we go in our lives. We belong in your presence, inside us and all around us.
Amen.

As a symbol of our belonging, we will share in this food and remember aloud the ways in which your presence has been made real to us in this day. Where did we notice, what did we feel, how did we take in Holy Presence?

Invite people to share in the food and conversation in a casual and relaxed way. Once the meal has been shared and the stories have been told, close with the following prayer:

Oh God of welcome, of home, of dark and light, and of belonging, be with us this night. Guide us safely home.
Amen.

THE SYMBOL OF THE CROSS

People wear a cross around their necks for a variety of reasons: as a way to profess their faith as a follower of Jesus Christ, or as a symbol of protection or a reminder of Christ's suffering, death and new life. Yet in many countries, wearing a cross and asserting Christianity is against the law. Wearing a symbol of faith and outwardly professing that faith is not something to take lightly.

Wearing the cross is an interesting and powerful adornment practice. It is the key symbol of the Christian faith. The following practice can be a powerful experience for a group to do during Lent and Easter.

 Hand out a cross to each youth at your gathering. Simple crosses are available at Christian bookstores or online. Perhaps there is a woodworker in your congregation that would make wooden crosses for each member of your group. Ask youth to hold their cross during the following conversation time.

Discuss the following questions together.

- *Where in our church do we see the symbol of the cross?*
  (A neat practice is to send youth throughout the church building to find all the crosses. Share the places in conversation following.)
- *What does the symbol of the cross mean to the people in our church?*
  Ask youth to interview people (at coffee hour following church for example) about the symbol of the cross and how they relate to it and use it in their life. Ask people if they wear a cross and what wearing it means to them. Have youth share the responses with the whole group.
- *Hold the cross in your hand and really look at it and seek to understand what the symbol of the cross means in your own life.*
  Share responses in small groups or in a whole group.

• What do you think are reasons that people wear a cross?

• Have you ever worn a cross and if so, why do you wear it?

Ask the group if they'd be willing to experiment with wearing a cross for a period of time (a day, a week, a month, depending on the group). Agree on the length of time together and ask people to notice how they feel while wearing the cross, who notices their cross, who asks about it, and what feelings they have when they are explaining why they are wearing it. After your experiment time is over, have a meeting to discuss the questions above and share more deeply what it means to share your faith in a public way.

MAKING THE SIGN OF THE CROSS

The sign of the cross is used primarily in Roman Catholic and Eastern Orthodox churches as a blessing. Generally, the practice involves touching the fingers to the forehead, sternum, left and right shoulder in that order as a way to acknowledge the connection with God. The following practice is a modification of the traditional sign of the cross that allows for freedom of expression. It also encourages contemplation on the meaning of this symbol.

Have the group sit in a circle or use this as one of the stations in a spiritual practices experience. Invite people to quiet themselves and find a still space within. Invite them to follow the leader's movements of making the cross in silence. Lead the traditional head, sternum, shoulder, shoulder cross first. After the pose rest hands in lap for a moment. Repeat the pose, rest. Repeat and rest. You may wish to have people choose four names for God that they can say to themselves at each stop: for example, head – Creator; sternum – Centre; shoulder – Jesus; shoulder – Christ.

You may also choose to make the cross in a different way by touching the top of the head, the solar plexus at the navel, one shoulder, then the other, crossing arms on the chest. Repeat three times with some silence to finish.

Following the practice, ask people to leave as they feel ready. Offer minimal conversation about the practice. Simply let people experience the way of making the sign of the cross.

PRAYER TO END THE CHAPTER

Oh God, Creator, I am aware. My living is full of moving: to catch a bus, to move a mountain, to encounter the world I need to move through it. I am aware now, but seek more awareness of how you move within my life. Help me to move, knowing, so I can really see. Amen.

CHAPTER **8**

COMPASSION

Love and compassion are necessities, not luxuries.
Without them humanity cannot survive. ~ Dalai Lama

Compassion is a response to need. It soothes a broken heart, calms trouble, and offers a cup of tea. Addressing the needs of ourselves and others with concern and love is part of being a committed human being and living life fully in God. When we take action for the well-being of ourselves and others we are taking the Biblical message of "do unto others as you would have them do unto you" to heart.

There is also tremendous power in reaching out by holding others in prayer. Responding to someone's needs with prayer takes compassionate action to a deeper place. Praying for another to be held in the love and grace of God and know peace of mind, body, and spirit brings you both to God.

The following practices are meant to awaken our inherent compassion by practicing intention, hope, and integrity.

I was THIRSTY

This personal reflection fits easily into a spiritual practices experience. You will need to have a glass of water and a lit candle on a table, and a chair to sit on. If people are working on their own, have the written instructions available.

I Was Thirsty

I was thirsty and you gave me something to drink

Matthew 25:35

Take a moment and focus on the glass of water on the table.

There are many people in our world who are thirsty for water to drink and for living water for the soul.

- How are you thirsty?
- What are you thirsty for?
- Who do you know who is thirsty?
- Who could you help by offering a drink of liquid or living water?

After you finish your reflection, say a silent prayer of blessing that all who are thirsty in body and soul will have their thirst quenched.

THE RIPPLE EFFECT

 This is a practice that can be used as a station in a spiritual practices experience or as a closing for a youth group meeting. You will need one or two small stones for each person present and a large shallow bowl filled with water. Place the bowl, the stones, a lit candle, and the outline (below) on a table.

If you are using the practice as a closing, invite people into the practice as below. Then ask them to come to the bowl one at a time and drop their stone into the water. Invite them to offer a word of gratitude for someone who has created ripples in their life if they wish.

The Ripple Effect

Pick up a stone and hold it in the palm of your hand. Feel its weight. Feel how it has been marked and shaped over time. This stone has been on the planet for millions of years.

Drop it into the water and watch the ripples that it makes. The stone's action causes the surface of the water to react. Keep watching until the water is still again.

Reflect on the ripples your actions have made in your life and in the lives of others. However small you may feel, the ripples of your actions go on and on and make a difference in others' lives that you cannot imagine or ever know. Remember someone whose actions made ripples in your life. How did those ripples affect your actions and the ripples you sent out? Offer a prayer of gratitude for someone who has created ripples in your life.

LIGHT a CANDLE

© Doris Kizinna

This practice can be set up as a station during a spiritual practices experience or as a permanent part of your youth room sacred space.

 You may already have a tea light stand. If not, create your own tea light holder by setting out a tray and filling it with sand. Place your stand or tray on a table beside a basket of tea lights, a Christ candle, and a taper candle to light the tea lights from. Have the following instructions available.

Light a candle for someone who needs a prayer

The light shines in the darkness and the darkness has not overcome it.

John 1:4, 5

Focus on someone you know who is struggling in a dark place who needs your prayers.

Say their name aloud to yourself and light a candle for them.

Offer God words for them.

Pray that light will overcome darkness in their life.

Your prayers on their behalf will make a difference.

PRAYING FOR THE WORLD

This is a practice of offering prayer for the places in the world where violence, conflict, and suffering are commonplace. Have youth create an image of the earth on a large piece of white paper or cardboard. Alternatively, use a large map or a globe (sometimes you can find globes in beach ball form). Have youth work together to create your planet Earth. Once Earth is complete, place it on table or floor so that the whole group can gather around.

Bring out a few copies of national and local newspapers. Have youth work in small groups clipping articles about situations that cause them concern. Then gather in a circle and share the stories, holding a moment of silence after each one. Place each clipping on the globe or map and then light a candle and place it on top of the clipping (if using a map) or on the table around the globe. End with a poem or prayer.

Oh Great Spirit, dear home Earth. We pray for the places we have read about. We are still when we hear of so much suffering. Help us find the small thing we can do with great love to bring wholeness to this planet home. Help us to hear your heartbeat and remember. Amen.

PEACE WALK

The ancient Buddhist practice of *metta* is the strong wish for and intentional focus on the well-being, safety and happiness of others. This exercise combines walking intentionally in silence with the loving-kindness practice of metta. I was taught the practice at a youth event many years ago. I also witnessed it at a Jubilee 2000 march in Cologne, Germany, where the G8 were meeting and people formed a human chain around the city centre to symbolize the bondage of Third World debt.

As I was making my way through the city, I passed a Buddhist monk standing still and silent at the fence that had been put up around the building where the world leaders were meeting. I stopped and noticed him. His lips were moving in prayer, and he was gazing intently at the building. His presence struck me and I watched him for a while before going to join the march.

Later that day, on my way back to the train station, I walked by the place where the monk had been and again stopped in my steps. He was still standing there silently, seemingly beaming metta into the hearts of the world leaders. I was amazed. His form of protest was so different from that of the hundreds of thousands who chanted and marched, yet it felt so necessary.

Recently I witnessed a similar silent protest. I was outside City Hall in a big American city and was faced with nine young adults protesting an injustice. They stood silently on the street, their mouths covered with duct tape. The image was strong and spoke volumes. They didn't say a word, but the image of them standing in silent peaceful witness is burned into my mind. The action of silent prayerful witness is a powerful way to practice non-violent protest and compassion.

This walking meditation allows you to slow and calm yourself, and has an impact on the situation you are praying for and the people who witness you. Your focus on praying for the well-being, and happiness of others will have an effect.

 Begin the practice with some words about the intention of the walk. Perhaps you are walking for peace; perhaps you are walking for the homeless in your town or city. If your goal is public witness, take the walk in a public area. You may wish to have the first person in line wear a sign outlining what you are undertaking. Walk for at least five minutes.

Have participants stand in a line, one behind the other, with a small space between them. Have each person place their right hand on the shoulder of the person in front of them. Have the first person in line begin to walk. Ask the group to step forward with the same foot as the leader. Get in sync with one another. Walk very slowly and walk together. Drop hands from shoulders and continue walking in rhythm.

In researching this practice, I noticed that there are peace-based witness walking meditations happening all over North America on a regular basis.

Peace be with you as you walk.

WELCOMING THE STRANGER

This practice encourages welcome and demonstrates how the action of welcoming can create community.

Read Hebrews 13:2. Reflect with the group on welcoming the stranger and how Jesus calls us to do so. Reflect on how our current culture is one of separation but in times past (and still today in many cultures) travellers relied on the open door of the stranger for shelter and sustenance. What would it be like in your town if it were common practice for a stranger to knock on someone's door seeking shelter and a meal because they had nowhere else to go? How would you respond? What would they do?

 Plan a barbeque on the grounds of the church or in a nearby park. Buy enough food and supplies for your group and ten extra people. Set a table beautifully, have music playing, and have the food prepared.

Have youth go out with a supervising adult and spontaneously invite ten people to attend the barbeque. These may be people out walking, or who live nearby, or they may be homeless. Sincerely offer them a meal with the youth group. You may be surprised at people's reactions and it may in fact be difficult to convince people to attend.

Alternatively, send out invitations to people who live in the neighbour-hood – people who aren't part of the congregation but who you know would appreciate sharing a barbeque with you. You might also invite people from a nearby shelter.

Share the meal in a simple and caring way. Allow your guests to feel honoured. Serve them first, take care of them at the table, offer them seconds, and make them feel super-welcome.

Once your guests have left, spend some time reflecting on what it was like to welcome someone.

I once took part in a practice of reaching out to street youth. We were asked to invite a homeless youth to come and have a piece of pizza with us. We were asked not just to buy the pizza and give it to them, but to go into a restaurant and eat and talk together. It was hard for some of us to embrace this practice of welcoming the stranger, but once we committed we found it to be amazing. The grateful and open conversation that happened was profound for the giver and refreshing I think for the person who received the pizza. In our giving and in our receiving we were equal in that time of sharing food.

RANDOM acts

In a culture that works hard at keeping us separate, simple acts that re-mind us of our common humanity can shift consciousness. We all have the power to make someone's day. This practice can also have implications for the people who receive, who may in turn decide to share a random act with someone else. Pay it forward, and voila, a heart is opened.

 Here are some simple ways to practice random acts of kindness and prayer:

- *Write anonymous notes of hope, kindness, and prayer, and leave them on benches, at bus stops, in library stalls, and public bathrooms. Put the notes in envelopes that say: For you. A special gift.*

- *Buy a big bunch of carnations and pass them out to people on the street, leave them on car windshields with a note, hand them out to business owners. Remind people to stop and smell the flowers, and wish them a good day.*
- *Go to a fast food restaurant and leave $5 to help cover the meal of someone else in line.*
- *Walk down a street and fill expired parking meters. Leave a small note on the window of the car saying the meter has been taken care of. Or do this practice anonymously.*
- *When a person is serving you in a restaurant or a store, strive to make a connection with them. Ask their name, tell them yours, ask how their day is going. Treat every person, especially those whose vocation is service, with respect.*
- *Visit seniors in a nursing home. Pair one or two youth with one senior and spend some time in conversation and caring together. Go for a walk or drink some tea together. Ask them about what it was like when they were a teenager and watch the stories roll.*
- *Set up a lemonade stand outside your church (or nearby) and offer free drinks to passersby. Simply give out the lemonade as a gift. Decorate the cups with words of prayer if you wish.*
- *Get to know your neighbours who live near the church. Drop by and say hello, offer an hour's worth of cleaning, raking, sweeping. Simply offer this as a random act. In the winter, gather together and shovel the walks around the church and the neighbourhood.*

Every time you do a random acts practice with your group, spend time reflecting on the experience and praying for the people who came across your path that day. Bring to mind the face of someone who passed you by and hold them in prayer. We don't fully understand how it works, but prayer can only help a situation or a person; another of God's deep mysteries at work in the world.

FORGIVENESS

Someone once shared with me that our call is to forgive everyone, everything.

How do we forgive when it seems impossible to do so? How do we embrace the one who caused us pain? How do we accept apology and move on, not necessarily forgetting, but letting go? These are challenges for the human being. How do we put aside our feelings and judgments and truly see that it is not only the other person who is full of troubles, faults, and has made wrong choices? Every person on earth needs to forgive someone (including themselves) and be forgiven. Perhaps we can see this as something that draws us together.

Forgiveness is not easy, but neither is not forgiving. Yet even if the forgiveness road seems too hard to follow right now, the beautiful thing is that it is always there, waiting for us to choose a life of fullness where we learn to forgive.

Katy Hutchinson's husband was killed when he went to break up a rowdy party in his neighbourhood in Squamish, B.C., on New Year's Eve, 1997. The 20-year-old man who committed the murder was convicted and sent to prison.

Katy did not want her children to grow up in the shadow of anger and regret over their father's death. Although her life had been deeply altered by the murder of her husband, Katy chose the hard path of forgiveness.

She chose not to perpetuate the pain of the situation and embraced the young man into her life, offering him hope for his future. She didn't forget what had happened, and held him to account for the murder of her husband, but she then moved to build a connection with him. She forgave him and allowed him to forgive himself.

He has since been released from prison and they give talks together to school and other groups about youth behaviour and forgiveness. Theirs is a powerful testament to what forgiveness means.

When Jesus was asked how many times we must forgive one another, he replied, "Seventy times seven." (Matthew 18:21–22) Practicing forgiveness moves us out of powerlessness into a life of freedom and wholeness. In South Africa, the Truth and Reconciliation Commission has been working with the practice of forgiveness with the goal of bringing wholeness to the country. Those who committed crimes and those affected by crimes are coming together to hear one another's stories, speak the truth, and seek forgiveness from one another. In hearing another's reality, there can be understanding on both sides.

Here in Canada, the government has apologized for its role in the suffering of aboriginal children who were sent away to residential schools. To acknowledge what has taken place and apologize for wrongdoing is the beginning of the process of forgiveness and the acceptance of life in all its fullness.

The practice of forgiveness deeply affects a person's well-being. In forgiving, we acknowledge that all of us need forgiveness. God's presence is with us in the moments of compassion and forgiveness.

What would it take for you to forgive seventy times seven? What would it take for you to be forgiven in that way?

SCRIPTURE REFLECTION ON FORGIVENESS

 This is a practice that could be a group or solitary prayer and reflection practice. Instruct people to read the following scripture once (or have someone read it aloud to the group). Then read it again, inserting your own name or the names of those present in the blank.

 As God's chosen one, holy and beloved, _____, clothe yourself with compassion, kindness, humility, meekness, and patience. Bear with one another and, if anyone has a complaint against another, forgive each other; just as the Lord has forgiven you, so you also must forgive. Above all, clothe yourself with love, which binds everything together in perfect harmony. (Colossians 3:12–14)

 Share in some conversation or journal on these questions.

- Imagine how your life would look if you lived the way the scripture calls us to live.
- Is there a situation or person you need to forgive?
- Is there a person you need to seek forgiveness from?
- How would you put love over everything else in your life?

 God, forgiveness is not easy. We are called to be people who love and forgive as we have been forgiven.
God of the Universe, help us let go of the petty parts of ourselves, the struggles of fighting, anger, disconnection, jealousy, and impatience. Guide us to be like light in the world, choosing always compassion, kindness, humility, gentleness, patience, and above all love. Thank you for your forgiveness, our worthiness, our life.
Amen.

LETTING GO INTO FORGIVENESS AT THE END OF EACH DAY

This forgiveness practice is similar to the *Ignatian Examen*, a practice of looking back over the day and reflecting through prayer (see chapter 5).

 As you prepare for sleep, let the events of the day go through your mind. Pay particular attention to places where you felt challenged, unfairly treated, at odds with someone, jealous, disliked, unheard, unacknowledged, or angry. Pay attention also to the places where you may have caused some of those feelings to arise in others. As you remember all those places, imagine letting them go. Use imagery of letting something go if that is helpful. Notice the places that require further attention – something that is hanging on, or something you need to ask for forgiveness for. Remember that today has passed and tomorrow is a new day, a chance to reconcile and make new. End your reflection with a prayer of gratitude for the places of joy and the places of conflict and what they have opened in you. Give thanks for choice, and for the chance to let go and begin again.

ADDRESSING SUFFERING WITH PRAYER

Most of us know what physical pain is. We also know what it's like to be hurt by words or have our heart broken. Some of the people that you minister to may have a greater experience and understanding of suffering than you. Most will have witnessed friends and family members experience pain. Some will have seen family members or friends die.

Something happens within us when we witness suffering in other beings regardless of what age we are. As humans, we have an inherent wish to alleviate the suffering of others. We are compassionate beings.

The bottom line is that life brings deep joy and it brings terror, and insulating people from that reality is a great dis-service. If we are living life in all its fullness, then looking at the shadows, the dark, the terror, and the pain is part of living such a life.

It is in the times of suffering and desperation that prayer seems to arise naturally. We cry out to God in our misery and despair. Prayer has a physical effect on pain and suffering. It calms and centres, and allows Mystical Presence to create space for an end to suffering.

Compassion calls us to move below the surface and understand what another person is going through, and through open sharing to soothe and comfort. Praying along the way helps. I don't know how it does – another one of life's mysteries – but it does.

If an emergency happens, our first response should be for the well-being of the individuals involved, but following that it is often a circle of prayer that calms those involved and allows them to cry out to God for help. Many people welcome a time of prayer following a scary event. Spontaneous prayer that clearly addresses what has occurred and asks for courage and presence in the midst of suffering, confusion, and concern can prove beneficial.

Below is a sample prayer for times of suffering and distress. I encourage you to go spontaneously into prayer and to be open to the movement of Spirit as she calls you into prayerful response.

 God who is with us in everything we do, be with us today as we face what is happening. Be with the people around us who are in pain and suffering, be with us all as we seek to be people of light in a time of darkness. Be with us God. Hold us all in your loving care.
Amen.

SERVICE LEARNING AND PRAYER

Many youth groups are involved with service learning. This practice engages youth with various needs in the world through projects or programs. Through their engagement with the world, youth learn more about themselves and their ability to make a difference. Taking on a service project manifests the gospel message of loving our neighbour as ourselves and is an experiential way of teaching that the actions of one person can make a difference.

 Whatever you choose to do with your youth ministry, it is vital to enter any practice of service or solidarity with prayer to guide and hold you throughout. Sometimes we will confront difficult situations (poverty, discomfort of others, lack of resources) in our service that are often best dealt first by prayerfully acknowledging that we are here simply to do small things with great love. Prayer before entering a new situation can ground people into the space so they will be able to respond. Prayer also bonds the group so they can depend on one another if help is required.

 Merciful God, help me live my life in merciful compassion. Let it flow from my heart out into the action of my hands and feet so that I live in the awareness of what I can give and how I can serve.
Help me stop for the hungry, the lost, the cold, the troubled.
Help my heart choose to bring love into action and silently bless the one who sits across from me, the one who walks toward me, the one who serves me. Honouring, blessing, living, being. The face of Jesus alive.
Amen.

Prayer before starting out on a service learning project

Oh God, be with us in our service, our awareness, and our understanding. The people we serve are you, and the people we serve are us. We name before you now our prayers of concern for ourselves and for one another as we enter into this project to make a difference. (Invite group members to go around the circle and offer aloud a word of prayer for themselves or others in the circle.)

Oh God, who has given us everything we need to be here now, help us remember that it is ultimately your hand that guides us. We give thanks for this opportunity to be of use.

Amen.

Prayer following a service learning project

Oh God of the universe, thank you for the chance to serve. Thank you for guiding us and helping us understand how important every single action is. We name before you now our prayers of concern for the people and situations we experienced today. (Have group members go around the circle and name aloud those people and situations they would like remembered in prayer.)

Oh God, as the faces of the people we met today pass through our minds, we ask your presence and peace with each one. Help us remember them when we are back in our daily routine. Help us remember that serving isn't just something we do as a special event but something to do every day. We are alive. We are here. We give thanks for the chance to be of use.

Amen.

SERVING THE WORLD

The practice follows a service project with a vigil/reflection.

 Set up an opportunity for service that addresses the issue of _____ (I have chosen homelessness here). It could be serving a meal at a mission church, making sandwiches and handing them out on the street, or volunteering with another group that works with the homeless. Be sure the opportunity allows participants to engage deeply with the issue and interact directly with those who are homeless.

Begin the practice of service with this prayer, adapting it to relate to the issue you are addressing:

 Holy Presence, be with us this day as we come face to face with people who are suffering in many ways. Guide us to act with compassion. Open our hearts. Help us to deeply appreciate the reality of all lives. May all people we encounter today find peace, stability, abundance, and joy. May we see the face of Christ in everyone, and may they see the face of Christ in us.
Amen.

 Following the service learning project, hold a vigil with the people who participated. Have a time of prayer for the suffering encountered as well as a time of reflection. You could invite others from the community to attend.

Have the vigil reflection set up in a quiet room with a lit candle on a central table. Have tea lights in votive holders around the Christ candle. Open the vigil reflection with the following prayer, then share the stories of the experience, framing the conversation with these questions: *Where today did you see suffering? Where did you see God's presence in the midst of suffering?*

After all have shared, invite people to come forward and light a tea light for someone they encountered, saying their name and offering any words of prayer they wish. Play quiet reflective music and offer people the opportunity to stay in the space in silent prayer and reflection for as long as they wish.

Make Me an Instrument of Your Peace

 Lord, make me an instrument of your peace.
Where there is hatred, let me sow love,
Where there is injury, pardon,
Where there is doubt, faith,
Where there is despair, hope,
Where there is darkness, light,
Where there is sadness, joy.
O Divine Master, grant that I may not so much
seek to be consoled as to console,
not so much to be understood as to understand,
not so much to be loved, as to love;
for it is in giving that we receive,
it is in pardoning that we are pardoned,
it is in dying that we awake to eternal life.

~ St. Francis of Assisi

CIRCLE OF COMPASSION

This is a mandala group practice where we name places and people that need our love and compassion. The mandala can be displayed in the church or youth room as a reminder of our call to seek justice, love kindness, and walk humbly with God.

    Have available a large circle of paper (see mandala practice in chapter 6). Begin with the prayer below and then invite people to add the names of people and places that need love and compassion to the circle with paint or felts. You may wish to have some newspapers or magazines available to cut words and images from.

Once the mandala is complete, attach it to a wall, gather together, and ask people to meditate on it while you play some quiet music. Ask people to choose one thing on the mandala that is of deep concern to them. Name those aloud. Then have people work in pairs to discuss why that issue is important to them. Have each person create a way to address their issue. Maybe it's something very simple like reading more on the subject, or talking to a specific person about the issue, or perhaps a larger project will arise, like a fundraising event, or travelling somewhere to witness. Have each person write out their goal and place those written words on the mandala somewhere. Not only is this a reminder for them to get at that goal, but it lets others know what that person is working on.

Encourage youth to come back to the mandala from time to time throughout the youth group year and check in on how the thing they chose to work with is influencing their lives. Encourage them to keep on with their goal or to set another if the first one no longer fits.

Spirit of Life, you give us a chance to love in everyday situations where there is suffering and pain. Let us be present to the moments when there are no words, there are only hands to hold, and tears to wipe away. In our open hearts we are changed when we really see below the surface of life. When we hold another's well-being as the object of our concern, we are blessed. Help us to stay present when we are uncomfortable or don't know what to do. Help us remember that our presence makes a difference, and that through our silent response great gifts can come.
Amen.

a prayer of compassion for one country

This practice models the Buddhist practice of acknowledging suffering with loving-kindness and compassion.

Put up a large world map in the youth room. Have people sit facing the map. Depending on the size of the group, you may need to have more than one map up in the room.

Invite people to calm and centre themselves and focus on the map as you say,

This is our world and it needs our compassion, love, and prayers. Let your eyes roam over the countries and cities, noticing where your eyes stop. Imagine the lives of the millions of people that live in this country or city. People with dreams and hopes as real as your own. Think of the way life is lived in this country and what challenges the people who live there face. Send warm thoughts of compassion there.

Provide pens and paper and ask youth to write down the name of the country or city they have focused on, and then write down a prayer to offer. Have people come forward one by one and say aloud the country's name and read their prayer. Then have them tape or tack their paper onto the edge of the map.

Leave the map up in the room you are working in and allow others to witness the prayers.

EMBRaCING HOPE

Hope is the combination of expectation and desire. Human beings seem programmed to hope. The Christian faith encompasses hope because of the promise that, "nothing can come between us and the love of God." In the midst of incredible strife, disaster, illness, wrongful imprisonment, abuse, and terror, we cling to hope.

There is story I would like to share about a community in the highlands of Guatemala that was used as a centre for torture during the civil war in the 1980s. The people there faced tremendous life-crushing events: murder, abuse, torture, and violence. When the war ended in 1996, life began to return slowly to this community, although it took a long time for people to want to come back.

The people of the community began rebuilding the church. They looked to the future with hope, but they could not and would not forget what had happened in their town. In the process of reconstruction, they uncovered a well behind the church that had been used as a pit grave. They also uncovered a cave just outside town where many more bodies had been left. The bodies were exhumed and gently prepared for burial.

On Good Friday a service was held outside the cave. The names of those who had been killed were read out in this way: *Andreas Gomez has died as Jesus has died.* On Easter Sunday, a service was held in the church that had been reconstructed. The words spoken held the hope of resurrection: *Andreas Gomez has risen as Jesus has risen.* In the midst of unbelievable suffering, there was cause for hope. A new way was possible. The living Christ was present in those who had died and risen again.

We are never separate from the love of God. People in affluent nations face struggles such as isolation and hopelessness. Although basic human rights and needs are met, the more complicated needs of community, love, and compassion are more difficult to attain. However, there are actions we can take as a community of faith that pull people away from isolation and hopelessness. We can form community with intention, praying for one another and living in connection, alive in Christ's body, each part vital to the whole. Teaching people that another way is possible is one of the thrilling parts of ministry with youth. Living in deep hope is one of the great gifts young people can give to the world. Your task is to find ways to access and share the gift of hope in a world desperate for it.

Be strong and courageous; do not be frightened or dismayed, for your God is with you wherever you go. (Joshua 1:9)

CHAPTER CLOSING PRAYER

Hope is a small thing, fragile and strong.
Smell hope on the water, taste hope on the wind.
Mover of mountains, ancient of days,
Reveal deep hope in us; guide us in your ways.
Amen.

CHAPTER 9

TOGETHER IN COMMUNITY

Draw the circle wide. Draw it wider still.
Let this be our song, no one stands alone, standing side by side,
Draw the circle wide. ~ Gordon Light[1]

Relational youth ministry focuses on how to connect in a faith community, how to know one another more deeply, and how to pull one another toward God. Practices of community gather us to focus on loving one another and the world as we draw closer to God. When we intentionally gather as a community in love and mutual awareness of our common connection we need to name it so that all who are present know it. The place we provide in youth ministry isn't only about being with friends, belonging to a group, fun, field trips, mission experiences, or special retreats. It is also about taking seriously each person's (including one's own) connection with the Divine. That can often be more easily nurtured when we belong to a community intentionally leaning toward life in God. Our practice grows stronger when we practice together. In a culture where many people feel disconnected and separate, being included in community is invaluable. It is a gift for youth to know they have a place at the table and in the circle, and that there are people who understand them and notice when they aren't around.

Welcome

We seek to embody the extravagant welcome of Jesus – a tangible and real practice that counters what our dominant culture offers. Throughout the Bible, Jesus clearly welcomes us: Follow me.

How we welcome in youth ministry is important. The way people feel when they first enter a space (say for a Sunday morning service or a youth group meeting) has everything to do with their level of comfort and continuing desire to be there. Remember that people make judgments about a new experience very quickly, and how they feel in the first few minutes of being in a new situation will have a lot to do with whether or not they will come back.

Think clearly about how you welcome people. Reflect on the ways your congregation practices welcome. How do you welcome people who are attending the youth program for the first time? How are you and the program seen by new people? How do you see them? Make a list to consciously plan your welcome strategy.

Practice welcome in ways that lead to further connection. Welcome is mainly a practice of acknowledging another person and their needs. Here are some ways to incorporate an intentional extravagant welcome into your youth ministry program.

- *When new members come to the youth program for the first time, greet them warmly when they enter the room and address them as they leave. Make a meaningful connection with them. Make sure they feel able to participate if they wish to. Check in with them during the meeting. Be attentive to them. Ask a seasoned youth group member to hang with them and take special care of them.*

- *Send a card to a new person during the week following their first meeting. Write it personally and mail it. No e-mails!*

- *Create welcome packages for new people. Include a meeting schedule, a prayer card of practices to do at home, some youth program memorabilia (t-shirt, button, etc.) so they can feel part of the team, a treat to enjoy later, a postcard written by some of the members thanking them for coming and welcoming them back, a prayer request card to bring back next time.*

- *Have a conversation with dedicated youth members about a strategy for welcoming people. Get their ideas and create a plan for extravagant welcome together.*

- *Post signs around the youth room that call for all to be welcome in this place. Have youth create the welcome statement together at the beginning of the youth group year. A sample sign may look like this:*

> **This is a place of welcome. It is a place that is different from the world out there. It's a place to be yourself. Everyone is welcome here. It doesn't matter who you are and how you come to the space. Bring your whole self here and be welcome.**

GATHERING IN COMMUNITY AROUND A TABLE

The practice of gathering around a table and sharing food is central to the Christian faith. There are many ways to share food and presence with one another, from the more formal practices of Communion and remembering the Last Supper, to gathering for a simple meal, to sharing a bag of popcorn on a walk in the park. All are ways to draw people together to celebrate life-giving sustenance for body and spirit.

There are many ways to share food within a youth ministry program. In fact, youth leaders have known for eons that food can be used as a tool to pull youth into the program. The classic youth pizza night has been a staple of youth ministry for years. Yes, youth love pizza. It's a fact. And I'd encourage you to look beyond pizza as the way you share food with youth.

 Below are some practices that will nourish not only the bodies but also the spirits of youth. As with the other practices in the book, your intention and the attention you pay to setting up a space is important. Consider doing more than just slapping the pizza boxes down on the table and inviting a free-for-all. Youth will notice that you have paid attention to the way their meal is set up. They will notice that you actually took the time to think of them and how they will enjoy the meal and time to-

© Doris Kizinna

gether. These practices also teach an alternative way of being in our fast food culture, where youth may rarely share a meal at a table with their family. These practices model sharing food and ourselves around a table as important and nurturing activities in a community of faith.

SAYING GRACE

Giving thanks before we eat is a simple and gracious act of prayer. If the same words and actions are used repeatedly, it can add to the feeling of ritual around mealtime. I'd encourage you to go beyond the classic *Johnny Appleseed* camp grace and try some new ways of showing gratitude. Some ideas:

- *Have youth create a youth group grace that you use regularly.*
- *Make a list of "old favourites" and post it on the wall in the youth room. Then it's easy to choose a grace when you need one.*
- *Invite a specific youth to be responsible for the grace for a particular meal. Allow them complete liberty in choosing and saying the grace. Ask them to either prepare a grace before the meal, or share one spontaneously at the meal. Check in with them the day before to make sure they still have it on their radar. Ask a different youth for each occasion.*
- *Encourage youth to practice saying grace at home. If their family doesn't share in grace, encourage them to introduce the concept and see if their family will practice with them at least some of the time.*

Some Graces to Use

Giving God, thank you for... (invite youth to share what we are thankful for)
With hands open, we receive... (cup hands together in front of heart)
With hands open, we then give... (cup hands and extend in front of body)
Giving God,
Amen.

We are here God. You are all around us, in everything we see and touch. We are thankful that in a world where many don't have food we have been given enough food for this day. Help us to see your face in everyone we meet. May others see your face in us.
Amen.

 Loving and giving God, we gather around this table of love. As we seek to connect with Mystery that created the universe, we touch deep places in our being. We savour the mystery and gift of a single day, holding tight the hands of those we love. We sing of the joy of living, we bow heads and give thanks, we hold hands around the table of plenty, and we give thanks. In a world where many are hungry, we are grateful for this abundance.
Amen.

COMMUNITY MEAL

Hanny, a youth ministry colleague, developed the concept of a community meal as the basis for her program with youth. She was concerned that the youth she worked with weren't being provided with adequate nourishment at school or at home so she decided to centre her weekly youth meetings on a meal. She provided some staples at the church (pasta, juice etc.) and youth would bring with them whatever they could. The group would then create a meal together with what they had. The meals were sometimes very simple, sometimes more elaborate. Following the meal, the group would walk to a nearby corner store and have slurpees.

This group was formed around the necessity of food for life. Cooking and eating together taught sharing, connection, tradition, simplicity, ritual, making the most of what you have, and cooperation.

To begin a community meal practice with your group, decide on the frequency (say once a month) and set the dates. Call youth the week before to remind them to bring something to share (whatever they have at home). Once everyone arrives, place all the food on the table and have a conversation about the meal you'd like to cook. Creating a unified theme from the diversity of items may call for some ingenuity, and having some staples on hand comes in handy at this point.

Get to work in small groups preparing the food. Have one group set the table, using candles, placemats, napkins, and perhaps flowers. Set out the food buffet style.

Just before eating, have everyone stand behind their chair and share in the grace. During the meal, either allow for free flow conversation or pose some questions to get people reflecting and talking. Eat the courses separately. Start with salad, then main course, then dessert. End the meal with everyone working together on cleanup.

MINDFUL eaTING

Food is essential to life and the practice of honouring it is one we can share with youth. In a world where many don't have enough to eat, it's our faithful duty to treat food with reverence and awe. It's never okay for food to be used in ways that are destructive or degrading, for games or a food fight tool. Beneficial practices include noticing how food tastes, how varied and delicious it is, how it brings people together, and how it sustains us. Find ways to bring conversation about the great gift of food into your ministry with youth.

WHERE DOES YOUR FOOD COME FROM?

 Read Genesis 1:29–31

 This practice can be done as part of a group meal. Lay out all the ingredients on a table and gather everyone around. Share a moment of silence and ponder the elements in the food – the water, the soil, the wind, and the sunlight contained in it. All good things, all gifts from God. Then have conversation about where each item came from: carrots from a farm down the road, avocadoes from Mexico, pasta from Italy, juice from South Africa. Read labels and make a list of all the places contributing to the meal. Give thanks for the abundance and diversity of food that the earth provides.

In the midst of our blessings, strive to remember those who have blessed us with food, and those who have laboured so that we are fed. We have more than we require. Our lives are overflowing with good things. Fostering a sense of deep gratitude for our blessings is a great gift to offer youth.

BAKING BREAD

Breadmaking with a group is quite easy. It just takes a little planning, and the period of waiting for bread to rise offers a chance to talk and connect. Depending on the size of the group you are working with, you may need to set up a number of mixing stations so that everyone has a chance to get their hands into the dough. Have no more than three people at each station.

 Begin with a prayer of thanksgiving (see below). Ask youth to call to mind a memory they have around sharing bread. Have some members of the group tell their stories. The rest of the group may share during the rising process. Give youth the breadmaking instructions and send them off to work in their teams. You may wish to work with one group or move around to answer questions or give assistance.

While the dough is rising, gather the group together to share in the rest of the memories. You may also wish to talk about breads from around the world and how bread is a gift of life. You may wish to purchase various types of bread and have an international bread buffet: tortilla from Latin America, pita from the Middle East, challah from Israel, baguette from France, naan from India. Share each type of bread and say a word about its use in its country of origin. Ask youth to imagine a person who might eat this kind of bread every day. Create an image of what life might be like for them. What challenges do they face? What brings them joy?

At the end of the international buffet, share a closing prayer (see below).

After the bread has risen, ask youth to shape the dough into shapes (loaves, braids, flowers, letters, bread sticks, etc.) before baking. Your group may choose to offer the baked bread for your church Communion service, or your own youth agape meal or Communion. Your group may wish to share it with those in your community who need bread, live alone, or are ill. (This of course means that the bread is of a quality that you are comfortable with giving away.) Your group may just decide to dig in and enjoy one of life's true pleasures – warm bread straight from the oven. Bread is more than just grain, water, salt, and yeast. It is a holy food, a miracle to be shared.

 God, give to us our daily bread, Creator of the universe, you brought from the earth food for our lives, the mystery of grain, water, salt, and yeast. For all the gifts that sustain us we are thankful.
Amen.

Give each person a piece of bread to hold during this prayer.

 This is bread. A holy piece of creation. A mystery of grain, salt, water, and yeast. This bread was baked with love and gratitude. We give thanks for this circle of friends to share bread with. We hold this bread knowing that God is with us in this bread, this community, this world. We pray.
Amen.

 This beautiful blessing comes from the Jewish tradition and is said before the eating of bread on Shabbat and other holidays. An action with this prayer is to hold the bread up in devotion and thanksgiving. Say together:

 Blessed art thou, Lord our God, Creator of the universe, who brings forth bread from the earth.
Amen.

COMMUNION

 Read Luke 22:14–20

Sharing Communion is one way to gather around a table in community. Different traditions have different ways in which to engage the practice of Communion. Connect with ordained staff (minister, priest, or pastor who has been called to administer the sacraments) in your congregation and ask them to assist you with Communion for your youth group.

Communion is an important Christian ritual. Sharing the bread of life and the cup of blessing is a way to remember Jesus and reach out to God and one another. Serving your own youth Communion or having them serve you can be a deeply meaningful practice. You may wish to use the practice of Communion as a special closing or as a regular youth group practice. Youth need to know that Communion is an accessible and self-nourishing practice.

There are many ways to share in this remembrance; again, intention and awareness of the message you are seeking to proclaim is important. You may wish to use intinction (the practice of tearing a small piece of bread from a loaf and then dipping it into the cup). You may wish to have people take a piece of pre-cut bread and eat it, then drink from the common cup. You may wish to pass a loaf of bread and a chalice of juice (some churches use wine for Communion) around the circle and have people serve each other. You may wish to have all the bread and juice on a central table and invite people to come forward and serve themselves and each other in a more spontaneous way.

All are welcome at this table. No matter who you are, where you have come from, and what you bring of yourself here today, you are accepted and welcome. We remember Jesus, who shared his life with others. Look around the room and notice the people who are standing with us here today (give people some time to look at others). *Jesus is here. Jesus used grain, water, and wine as symbols of love, community, presence, and meaning. He lived a life of depth, and he calls us to do the same. We ask the Spirit of Life to come into this place and into this bread and juice so that it is not only bread and juice for our bodies but nourishment for our souls.*
We share this bread of love and friendship (break the loaf in two) *and this cup of mystery and life* (hold up the cup). *This is the bread of blessing and the cup of life.*
Amen.

aGaPe MeaL

In most traditions, it is only the ordained minister who officially leads Communion. This isn't always practical, especially if you wish to introduce the concept of sharing a special meal of faith with youth on a regular basis and the ordained staff isn't part of your regular youth meetings. The alternative is an *agape* meal. *Agape* means love in Greek and an *agape* meal can be described as a feast of love. When we intentionally engage in an *agape* meal, it brings to mind the meals that Jesus shared with his friends and how we are united in his spirit. The first Communion that Jesus shared was probably held around a dining table where friendship, laughter, good food, and drink were present.

Reliving that Last Supper can be a radical community building practice. It makes gathering in joyful community in the presence of God real and relevant. Unlike most Communion services in church, spontaneity and informality are the keys for an *agape* meal, where anyone can lead. You could frame the meal around a service or just state the intention at the beginning and allow people to share food and community in the ways that they will.

 Tonight we remember the meals that Jesus shared with his followers. We remember the loaves and fishes, the wedding feast, the dusty meals on the side of the road. We remember the meal he shared the last time he was with his friends. We know that this bread is more than just bread when shared in community. It becomes food for our journey, and love for our way. May we share this bread and this meal on this night and know that we are all one in Jesus. Amen.

Deep Listening

Our world offers few opportunities for people to speak about their lives and their personal faith in a deep way with others. Ideally, being in community means being known, heard, listened to, understood, and valued. Being known allows self-esteem, personal worth, and awareness of self to flourish. Allowing for that in a youth ministry program is an important gift to youth.

This activity is best done with a group of older youth who have established trusting relationships with each other, or on a retreat when there is time to build strong community before the practice. It's possible that there may be some people who don't feel comfortable sharing. Please stress that people are welcome to share whatever they wish and that this is not a place of judgment, rather one of listening and acceptance.

 Being known in community involves letting people into your life and your story, moving beyond surface conversation to conversations that matter. Connect people in groups of three. The goals are to listen well and be listened to.

Prior to the listening experience, have youth spend some time journalling, focusing on three questions:

- *What do I like about my life?*
- *What do I want to change about my life?*
- *Where do I see God in my life?*

 Share an opening prayer with the whole group. Explain the parameters of the practice and ask people to begin by sitting in their small group for a minute of silence. Then invite people to share their responses to each of the questions within their small group, one person at a time. Two listeners will focus on the one speaking, making no comments. Each speaker will be given five minutes. If the person is done speaking at two minutes, space will be held for them until their five minutes is up. Often people think they are done after a few minutes and don't know what else to say, Given time and space a person will often come up with other things to say during the silence. The leader will keep track of the time. When the first five minutes is up, the group will sit in silence for one minute. Then the listeners will thank the speaker and offer back one thing they heard that struck them. They will simply reflect back what they heard and how it resonated with them.

When all three people have spoken and been heard, ask each group to end with a prayer for the group. You may either lead them or have them pray themselves.

At the end of the practice, have the whole group sit in a circle and spend a short time reflecting on what it was like to be listened to in this way. Have each person offer a prayer in silence or aloud for the two people that they listened to. Once everyone has had a turn, the leader closes the practice.

LAYING ON OF HANDS

 Read 2 Timothy 1:6

The practice of laying on of hands has been part of the Christian faith since the very beginning. The laying on of hands is a blessing. Jesus often laid his hands on people in healing and recognition. Using the practice in a youth ministry context is a powerful way to pray together and joins us with a long line of the faithful who have done the same, and with the Holy Spirit who we call on to move in our lives. Laying on of hands is also used in healing ministry to call Spirit to intercede and heal the energy flow throughout the body.

You may wish to use the practice of laying on of hands when someone from the youth program requires a special blessing or is leaving the youth group. Sending people off with a blessing of prayerful touch can offer a deeply spiritual ending. You may also wish to lay hands on each person in the group in turn, offering words of blessing and celebration.

Prayer for Someone Leaving

 Invite youth group members to gather around the person to be blessed and lay their hands on the head or shoulders of the person. Offer a prayer for the person being blessed. Notice their gifts and what they have brought to the group, and acknowledge what they are going to and how they will go.

 *Loving God, we ask that your spirit live and work in the life of
_____, that wherever they go they will know that this community cares for them. They are not alone. Be with them as they
_____, serving the world and the people around them with love and humility. Loving God, we ask your blessing on this life, keep
_____ in your care.*
Amen.

Prayer for Ending a Youth Retreat

This practice focuses on the laying on of hands on each person in the group before the group ends a significant time together or departs for summer or other extended break. It's best done with a group that isn't too big as this practice can take some time. If working with a large group you could create smaller circles of blessing.

 Each person who wants a blessing steps into the middle of the circle. The others lay hands on that person and some words are spoken. Generally we lay hands on the shoulders, head, and back of the person being blessed.

Spirit of Life, we thank you for bringing _____ to be a part of this group. We give thanks for all the blessings _____ has brought to us all (allow space for people to share a word about the person). *We ask a blessing on this life. We ask that your spirit live and work in _____'s life until we are together again.*
Amen.

appreciation

There is a story that I once heard about a Roman Catholic priest who dedicated his life to teaching. He went about his work in quiet and reserved ways. One day, when he was quite old and long retired, a former student came to see him. The student expressed to the teacher his gratitude for all that he had done for him. The priest started to cry. The student was taken aback, and asked what was wrong. The priest replied that it was the first time in his life that a student had personally thanked him for his work. He was deeply touched and moved to finally know for sure that he had made a difference.

Thanking people is an important practice that builds awareness and esteem in us and others. It's important to teach the practice of appreciation to youth and to give youth the opportunity to thank one another, their leaders, and others. Listed below are some ideas on ways for youth to show appreciation.

Appreciation Postcards

Ask youth to write anonymous or signed postcards to their friends, family, youth group members, or people they admire but don't know personally, offering gratitude for their encouragement, service, kindness, inspiration, and support. Have youth write the postcard, address it, and add the stamp. Practice this once a month with your youth group so that practicing gratitude becomes a ritual.

Gratitude Circle

Allowing people to write or share aloud their appreciation for each other is a good practice for the end of a youth group year or important youth event. Spoken appreciation creates intimacy. Written appreciations/gratitudes are a wonderful way to give youth something to take with them as a way to remember and cherish the kind words of others. I know one youth who has kept every note of affirmation that she has ever received in a special box. She takes them out and looks at them from time to time to remind her that she is loved. Sharing gratitude and affirming gifts deepens community, builds self-esteem, and practices the art of appreciation.

Gratitude Ceremony

Choose a day during your youth group year to focus the meeting on gratitude. Offer a gratitude ceremony where each person is given an award for the special pieces of themselves they bring to the group. Have people dress up in fun and wacky costumes, have a banquet, honour special youth group volunteers, honour the paid staff at the church, give thanks to God for the gift of the people around you. Make it a big, bold, celebratory event. Alternatively, plan a Sunday service focused on gratitude for the services people offer to the youth ministry program. Base the sermon on gratitude, offer a practice of laying on of hands and blessing for people's continued commitment, have people deliver testimonials on how a particular person or the church has made a difference in their lives, share songs of thanksgiving, share prayers on behalf of all those who serve in the congregation.

SABBATH

We live in the era of too much: too many physical possessions that require maintenance and care; too many hours of work, school, and after school activities; too many obligations, e-mails, tasks, and strains. The kind and amount of stress that most people face in their daily lives would have been incomprehensible to the generations before us. We are living hard and fast and it takes its toll through broken relationships and physical and mental illness and stress. The practice of Sabbath can bring rest and renewal so that we can cherish our blessings.

Sabbath can mean different things to different people. Ideally it is a time set apart to rest from things associated with work, success, busyness, and getting ahead. It's a time to chill out, hang out with people you like to be around, recharge, pray, and be close to God through people and nature. Sabbath takes us into renewal and rest, so we can discern what is really important in life. Sabbath practiced in community holds us accountable to one another and to our call to Sabbath.

 Here are some Sabbath practices you may wish to bring to your youth programs.

- *Spend some time talking with your youth about what Sabbath is and how it can be kept. Make a list of what to say yes to on the Sabbath and what to say no to. Say yes to music, worship, laughter, friends and family, napping. Say no to shopping, working,*

e-mailing, and using a car. Invite people to set one Sabbath goal to focus on during the next month. After a month, check back in to see how the practice went.

- *Invite a Jewish person to come and explain the practice of Shabbat, which is the Hebrew word for Sabbath. Have them come and share some of the rituals of Shabbat, like the Shabbat meal. How is it lived out and how does it make a difference to them in their lives? Allow space for youth to participate in the ritual if appropriate and allow time for questions and sharing following the conversation with your guest.*

- *Invite members of the congregation to come and talk with the youth about ways that they practice Sabbath, a kind of Sabbath panel discussion. Follow the discussion with a Sabbath feast for everyone.*

- *Challenge people not to wear a watch (or check the time on their cell phone) on the Sabbath. Let one day of the week not be ruled by the clock. Eat when you are hungry, sleep when you are tired. Incorporate this practice into a youth retreat.*

- *Invite the whole congregation to attend a spiritual practices experience one Saturday evening as the sun is setting. Liaise with youth to create the space and choose practices. Invite people to pray and practice faith together, focusing on the way the practice takes us into Sabbath. Allow at least an hour for people to move through the stations and then gather all together to share in a short prayer to call the Sabbath in. Ask people to intentionally think about how they will keep Sabbath. What will they not do? What will they incorporate for a day of balance, rest, and renewal? Keep the practices set up for use on Sunday morning before or after church as a way of continuing the focus on Sabbath. Save clean up so that no one is working on the Sabbath.*

- *Create a space for Sabbath at your youth events. Ask people to unplug from technology during part or all of the event. Have a cell phone check at the door, ask people not to bring iPods or computers with them. Create a space that is as free as possible from those distractions. When we don't have technology there to interact with, we turn to those around us. This strengthens your community and brings about a letting-go of the world "out there."*

REMEMBERING THOSE WHO HAVE DIED

Our culture makes it easy to live as though we will never die. But by not paying death any attention, we are missing out on understanding a big part of living: our ending. How are we living life in all its fullness if we are denying the fullness of life's ending?

You may be called upon to look death straight in the face and thus come to understand what it means in your life and in the lives of the youth you work with. You will almost certainly be called upon to help people through times of mourning and lingering grief following a death. A friend's mother died recently and as I reflected back on the experience, I was astounded to realize that I didn't see a person die until I was 37 years old. I thought that if I had been born in a place like Africa, I would have witnessed death many times over by that age, and more fully integrated the process of dying into what it means to live.

Wherever you are in your acceptance and experience of death, it's important to be able to talk about the issue with others and comfort those who are grieving. It's a big part of ministry with youth and a big part of youth pastoral care. I'd encourage you to take a course on the subject of death and dying or on pastoral care with people in grief. Remember that you will not be alone in accompanying people through grief. If you ever feel like you are facing something you can't handle, please know that there are others who can help you deal with your ministry in this context.

This practice remembers those who have died. It allows youth to ask and share what they need to about the subject of death. Please note that this practice may bring up intense feelings, memories of people they have lost, and questions they have about death. It is important to make time after the practice for people to transition and talk to someone if they need to. Please be sure to set up a way for that to happen. Be sure to name that option at the close of the practice and to check in the next day with youth who may have had a particularly hard time. This practice is intended to give youth a way to speak about a part of them that doesn't often get acknowledged. It's also a way into honest and open sharing of one another's stories.

 Create a comfortable and safe space – say a room in the church, or part of the sanctuary. Set out a circle of candles (unlit) around the Christ candle that will be lit when people have arrived.

Presente

This practice comes from Latin America. It was originally used to give people strength in times of war when many friends and family were lost to death squads and torture. It gave hope and strength and a sense that their loved ones were with them in their struggle.

The practice of *presente* reminds us that the people we name, although they have passed, are present with us here and now. *Presente* is Spanish for present.

 Ask youth to write down or prepare to name aloud those they wish to remember during the practice. As each name is spoken or read out, the whole group will say the word *presente* in unison. With each name, the person who wrote or spoke the name will come forward and light a candle for that name. Hold silence in the space while the candle is being lit.

The Remembrance Service

 Have soft music playing as people enter into the room. Invite people to settle into the space.

 Opening Scriptures: Matthew 5:4; Revelation 21:4; and John 8:12

 Share an appropriate poem or song.

Prayer

 We are here to remember those who have touched our lives in some way who have died. We remember those we have known and loved, those who have influenced us with their life and work, and those who are saints. We give thanks for their lives and know that they are present with us.

    We remember those who are presente *to us.*

Names are read or spoken. After each name, the whole group says the word *presente*. Hold silence as the person who wrote or spoke the name comes forward and lights a candle for the one named.

Closing

 Each one special, each one a gift. We remember all these saints, friends, and family, those who touched our lives. Those who are no longer on earth but who are with us still, present to our lives. You are welcome to sit and be in this space for as long as you would like.

You are welcome to join us in the next room for refreshment and quiet conversation. If you'd like to talk, there are people here who can listen. Peace be with you all.
Amen.

 Quietly play recorded music (see resources section) in the background and allow people time for personal reflection and prayer.

HeaRT TO HeaRT

This is a prayer to use as a closing for a meeting or as a way to deepen group connection. It is a practice of praying for self and other, and links a group physically and spiritually.

 To begin, have the whole group stand close together in a circle.

Take a deep breath in and out and place your left hand over your heart. Close your eyes if you wish. Feel the warmth of your heart where your hand is. Breathe deeply. In your own mind, offer a prayer for yourself, and what you may need on this day. (Time of silence for personal prayers.)

Take your right hand and place it on the (left) shoulder of the person on your right. Feel your connection to this person, and in your own mind offer a prayer for their well-being and peace. (Time of silence.)

Notice how we are standing in this circle of connected hearts. Feel the energy and warmth of these connected people. Offer a silent prayer for the life of this group. (Time of silence.)

This is a circle of friendship, this is a circle of energy, this is a circle
where God's presence moves in mysterious ways. In this circle of
care, in love and friendship, we give thanks.
Amen.

FOOTWASHING/HANDWASHING

The practice of washing another's feet and hands as a way to show acceptance and love comes to us from Jesus. In John 13:12–17, Jesus spends one of his last evenings on earth sharing a meal with his followers. Just as the meal is served, he does an odd thing for the times. He gets up from the table, and begins to wash the feet of his friends.

This intimate action of Jesus amplified his essential message of servanthood, love, and equality. Touching people, bowing down to them, taking on a woman's task, and giving as one of his last commandments that we should wash other's feet to show that no one is greater than another are profound examples indeed.

The foot or handwashing practice below is an intimate practice; people may feel vulnerable and moved when touched with love and compassion. At First United Church in Vancouver's downtown eastside, people offer footwashing and foot care to those whose home is on the street. The homeless are cleaned and blessed by this practice of care and servanthood. Holy Week, particularly Maundy Thursday, is a good time to parallel the practices that Jesus shared with his disciples. The group undertaking the practice should be mature enough to take it to heart and care for one another in this way.

 Have a number of stations set up around the room with a large bowl of warm water and a towel at each. People will work in pairs washing one another's feet. If your group is small, you may wish to sit in a circle and pass the bowl around, focusing on one person at a time. You may wish to have a few stations set up for people to come and simply receive footwashing from those whose task it is to wash feet. You may choose to substitute handwashing for footwashing. Handwashing may feel less risky and be easier to do with youth who feel self-conscious about taking off their shoes and letting someone touch their feet. Have a small feast of bread, cheese, and fruit ready to share as part of the practice, and set it out on a central table.

 Sing an opening song of your choice.

 Compassionate God, our feet are dusty from travelling the road of our lives. We come into this space seeking sanctuary and care. For gifts from the earth, we give thanks. For lives of service and compassion, we give thanks. For food to nourish our bodies and souls, we give thanks. For water and towels, symbols of cleansing and compassion, we give thanks. For Jesus Christ, his life among us, we give thanks.
Amen.

 Read John 12:1–3 and John 13:12–17 and then hold a time of silence.

Share in the footwashing.

When all have been washed, gather around the central table and serve one another food. You may wish to sit around the table or in a circle elsewhere. Share some conversation about the ways your youth group can continue to serve one another.

Water has been poured, bread has been broken, compassion laid out like a blanket, dusty feet cleansed, and we are strengthened to love and serve one another. Stay with us God, as we stay with one another on this journey in community.
Amen.

 Close with a song.

TWENTY DAYS OF GRATITUDE

The 20 days leading up to Thanksgiving is a great time to undertake this practice, as it will culminate in a celebratory Thanksgiving feast. As with any practice, this one takes some discipline to make it happen. Have each youth create their list of 20 ways for 20 days to give thanks at a meeting before the practice. Ask them to hold one another and you accountable to the practices, perhaps by sending e-mails to one another or a text message check-in if they complete the practice for the day.

At your Thanksgiving feast spend some time reflecting on the gifts that 20 days of focused gratitude have brought to your life. I've made some suggestions for ways to give thanks; you may have other ways related to your own life that you wish to use. Begin!

Day 1 *Say grace at all the meals you have today, no matter where you are and who you are with.*

Day 2 *Walk slowly around the outside of the building you live in and reflect on the memories that this dwelling contains. Give thanks for all that has happened inside and outside these walls, and for shelter in a world where so many have no home.*

Day 3 *Remember someone whose ministry you appreciate and call their office after hours and leave a message of gratitude that specifically outlines how you are grateful for their ministry.*

Day 4 *Write a note of gratitude to someone you know and send it to them.*

Day 5 *Walk through your neighbourhood slowly, and pay attention to all the people you see. Offer silent prayers of gratitude for their peaceful and neighbourly presence in your life as you pass them.*

Day 6 *Clean your kitchen with special care. As you clean, give thanks for the luxury in which you live, when so many around the world cook outdoors over a small fire.*

Day 7 *Pull out a photo album that you haven't looked at in a long while and savour the photos and the memories. Give thanks for the special memories you have.*

Day 8 *Write a letter of appreciation to the author of the book that has most influenced you.*

Day 9 *Consciously thank all people who serve you today: waiters, cashiers, gas attendants. Heartfully offer thanks for the way they use their life to make yours easier.*

Day 10 *Send an anonymous card of gratitude to someone you know. If you can, send flowers.*

Day 11 *Bake a loaf of bread or some cookies to give to someone you are grateful for.*

Day 12 *Take your best friend for a walk, and talk to them about the positive ways they affect your life.*

Day 13 *If you can, phone your mother and thank her for giving you the gift of life. If you can't make contact with her, thank her aloud anyway.*

Day 14 *Lay out in the sun. Let the warmth wash over you. Give thanks for the gift of life the sun brings.*

Day 15 *Give your pet a special walk or treat and tell them how important they are in your life. If you don't have a pet, borrow one from a friend.*

Day 16 *Look around your room and notice all the things that you have. All the useful tools. All the beautiful things. Really look at them. Are you treating them with respect? Clean up your space and reverently take care of all you have been given.*

Day 17 *Look at yourself in a mirror. Unique. Give thanks for the gift of your body, all its wonderfully made parts, all of you.*

Day 18 *Read a poem or a story and tell someone else about it. Read it aloud to someone and pass on the gift of the words with gratitude.*

Day 19 *Cook your favourite meal and invite a friend to join you. Give thanks before the meal, savour and enjoy the meal with your friend.*

Day 20 *Create and plan a Thanksgiving feast where people have the chance to offer gratitude for their lives. Prepare a simple or extravagant meal, appreciating all the while the many gifts your life holds. Find ways to honour those who are attending. Say grace and offer everyone an opportunity to speak a word of gratitude.*

THANKSGIVING FEAST

Start a tradition of sharing Thanksgiving with your youth group. Thanksgiving is the time of harvest and feast, the time for gratitude for the good great gifts of the earth. It's a time to be with people you care about and are thankful for. Thanksgiving is also a time to see firsthand the gifts of the earth through the harvest.

 Plan ahead for an evening feast. Organize youth into small groups of two or three to plan, shop, and prepare one course of the feast (appetizer, salad, entrée, dessert, beverages). Spend the day before the feast gathering food items, perhaps going to a farm and/or farmers market. Have youth do the purchasing. Encourage them to choose local food from local businesses. Spend the following afternoon at the church or at a home working on the various courses. Set a time for the meal to begin. Encourage people to dress up – create a sense of occasion. As the leader, focus on setting up a space that is warm and inviting, like a family thanksgiving table. Add special touches so that the space is welcoming and festive. Have candles on the table.

On the evening of the meal, have all the food set out and ready to serve. Ask everyone to sit around the table. Share in the simple prayer/

grace below to begin. Invite people to hold hands and look around the circle at the people and at the table. Light the candles on the table.

Gathering God, you have gathered us here in this circle of care and friendship. We give you great thanks for the people around the table, for the food in a world where many go hungry, for the rich plenty that the earth provides. We give you great thanks that today our needs for community, food, water, and compassion are met around this table of thanksgiving. We give thanks for the plants and the animals who have given so that we may be fed. We give thanks for the many people who were involved in bringing us this feast; those who planted, nurtured, transported, prepared, organized, and cooked this meal. We know that we are in the midst of many blessings. Thank you God.
Amen.

Have youth serve themselves one course at a time. Enjoy the meal together. During the meal, you may wish to pose a question in order to generate conversation, such as:

- *Tell us about the best meal you ever ate.*
- *Tell us about a time when you were welcomed around a table for a meal.*
- *Share a family Thanksgiving tradition.*
- *Talk about where this food came from, or the challenges and joys of working together to provide this meal for one another.*

When all are finished, share in a blessing on the meal and on one another. Have people offer aloud words that reflect the gratitude in their hearts.

To the God who blesses us we give thanks. Thank you for _____
(invite sharing of words).
To the God who does all these things, who brings us around this table of friendship, who blesses us in many ways, we give thanks. Amen.

passing the peace

The passing of the peace originates in the New Testament, mostly in the writings of St. Paul, and was practiced in the early church during the liturgy as a way of connecting and joining the gathered as the Body of Christ. While St. Paul suggested we pass the kiss of peace, today we tend to pass the peace of Christ through a warm handshake or an embrace. The passing of the peace is generally practiced during a Sunday morning service, but can be used in any service or gathering. It's a way of practicing love for one another, and a way to really see and greet the other person and wish them the deepest blessing, the peace of Christ.

Read John 20:19–21 and share the history and meaning of passing the peace.

Encourage youth to pass the peace to one another at different times during your gatherings. Suggest they try out passing the peace in a few ways: shaking hands, embracing (if they feel comfortable), holding hands in prayer pose and bowing to one another, or holding both hands of the other person. In each pose, ask people to look at the other person and say, "The peace of Christ be with you." In sharing the peace of Christ in this structured way, no one is left out and all are welcome to participate as they wish.

1 Words and music by Gordon Light, Copyright Common Cup Company, 276 Chester Court, Coquitlam BC, V3K 5C3 Canada. Used by permission.

CHAPTER 10

WORSHIP SERVICES

God is spirit, and those who worship him must worship in spirit and truth. ~ John 4:24

The practice of worship is to offer intentional praise, homage, or reverence to God. It's a time to focus our whole selves on opening our hearts.

Worship can take many forms. Some say that each moment of being in the world is an act of worship and connection with the Divine. Others find that directed worship in community is the place where God's presence is most accessible.

This chapter contains practices of communal worship suitable for a youth ministry program. The simple half-hour services are open to adaptation. I also encourage you to create your own practices of worship with your youth group. Creating worship is the practice of worship in itself.

WHO DO YOU SAY THAT I AM?

Gather images of Jesus (books, online, children and youth drawings, icons). Either print out the images and mount on cardstock, or create a Power-Point slide show. Have on-screen images looping and playing throughout the service and/or have hard copies spread around the worship space (on the central worship table, on the seats, on side tables). Have at hand a prayer bowl or worship bell. Have a Christ candle and some images of Jesus on a central table or altar.

Opening Words

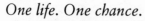

One life. One chance.

Jesus lived on the same earth as we do. He was born, grew through childhood, had a life and a ministry, was judged and killed. He rejoiced, celebrated, questioned, and suffered. He asked his followers, "Who do you say that I am?" And he asks that question of us over 2,000 years later.

Jesus asks, "Who do you say that I am?"

Enter into a time of silence. In this silence, choose one image of Jesus and let whatever thoughts arise in response to the image be with you. We will sit in silence for a few minutes and I will ring the bell to bring us back to this circle.

Choose a song from your tradition that speaks of the life of Jesus.

Read Matthew 16:13–15, or have one of the youth read the scripture.

Response

 Hand out a strip of paper with a scripture phrase about Jesus printed on it (see below for examples) to each person, along with a pen and paper.

In the beginning was the Word, and the Word was with God, and the Word was God.

John 1:1

~~~~~~

And she gave birth to her firstborn son and wrapped him in bands of cloth, and laid him in a manger, because there was no place for them in the inn.

Luke 2:7

~~~~~~

The child grew and became strong, filled with wisdom; and the favour of God was upon him.

Luke 2:40

~~~~~~

All of them asked, "Are you, then, the Son of God?" He said to them, "You say that I am."

Luke 22:70

~~~~~~

Moved with compassion, Jesus touched their eyes. Immediately they regained their sight and followed him.

Matthew 20:34

~~~~~~

The Father and I are one.

John 10:30

Ask youth to reflect on their phrase and write a one- or two-line response, reflecting on who they say Jesus is. Share the scripture phrases and responses during the following prayer.

 God of wonders, we are here. You are here. We are connected through so many things. You are alpha and omega, beginning and end. There is nowhere that is apart from your presence. You brought Jesus into this world – messenger, prophet, messiah, saviour, guide. We remember Jesus, who was _____ (share responses).
We thank you for life, for a path to follow that is full. Grant us peace and assurance that we are known and loved as Jesus was. Amen.

 Choose a favourite song that speaks about the life of Jesus.

WATeR IS LIFe

 Preparation

- Hand out a glass half full of water to each participant. Have them keep it close by during the service.
- Have a low table set up in the centre of the circle. Pile some rocks on it and balance a large clear plastic or glass bowl on top.
- Have a pitcher of water beside the bowl.
- Have an unlit Christ candle on the table.
- Have people sitting in a circle around the central table.

 Choose a song from your tradition that speaks either about gathering people together or the natural world (see resources section).

Litany

 Have one person read the litany below. While it is being read, have another person pour the water very slowly from the pitcher into the bowl. Pour slowly and intentionally, pausing occasionally during the reading.

Light the Christ candle.

Creator of all things, you swept over the waters.
The waters below and the waters above, mysterious life in liquid form, catching light, holding life. You were there.
Water flowed from a rock in the desert, a miracle.
A woman pulling water from a well, sharing living water.
Water of cleansing, baptism, new life in you.
Tide, sea, salt, sweet, stream, river, lake, cloud, flowing, moving over all the earth.
Circling the planet a thousand times, water never ending, just changing form.
Water turned to wine, water used to wash tired feet, water as servant.
The water of today circling round the planet in cloud and rain, river and ocean,
the same water that circled 2,000 years ago, 10,000 years ago, longer.
The water of today, strength for our path. The water of today, at risk.
Over and over, thank you for this gift of life.
Parched throat soothed, heart open, receiving.

 Choose another song.

Response

 Invite youth to hold the glass of water and reflect on the ways water touches their lives daily. After some moments, ask them to turn to a neighbour and share their responses.

 Jesus talked about living water. Living water is water for the soul. How do you experience living water? What is living water for you today?

Ask youth to sit silently with the questions for some moments and then offer them a chance to share aloud how they experience living water.

Once all who wish to have shared, end with a prayer and a song.

Invite people to join you in taking a drink of water during the prayer.

 Gracious Giver of Life, we thank you for nourishing our bodies, sustaining us and giving us life (drink water).
We give thanks for the way you are revealed in the stories, images, and water in our lives (drink water).
Soothing, thirst-quenching, cleansing, life-giving (drink water).
Giver of life, surround us, reveal the places of living water.
Each time we take a drink of water may we remember your presence in and around us.
Amen.

Jesus Calling

 Opening Song: *Calling God*, by Jan Arden.

 Play the song as a call to worship. Set the space with a Christ candle and have paper and pens for each person present. Hand them out before the service begins.

Light the Christ candle and offer a time of silence.

 Oh God who calls us, we open to another day of life. We open to this new day breathing life into us. This new day we call God, and God calls us; we call Jesus, Jesus calls us. Be present, be open, be love. Listen deep and long, for the great turning of life toward light is happening all around. Jesus says be aware, be open, be present, be love.

Amen.

 Choose a song (see resources section).

The Word

 Jesus says, call me, love me, know me, ask me, seek me, remember me, follow me.

Jesus says, when you pass through the waters, I will be with you.

Jesus says, the kingdom of God is inside you and all around you. Split a piece of wood and I am there, lift a stone and you will find me.

Jesus says, blessed are you when you are at the end of your rope, for you shall be saved.

Jesus says, I have called you by name and you are mine.

Jesus says, blessed are you when you hunger for justice, for you will be filled with justice.

Jesus says, rise up and be healed.

Jesus says, blessed are you when you are a peacemaker, for you will be called a child of God.

Jesus says, follow me.

Jesus says, blessed are you when you are persecuted because of me. You will inherit all of God.

Jesus says, follow me, call me, love me, know me, ask me, seek me, remember me.

What is Jesus saying to you today?

Reflection

 Allow some time and space for people to reflect on this question: *If Jesus could talk to you personally today, what is the message he would give you?* Then have each person write out the words that Jesus would offer them. Begin with the words, *Jesus says.* Have the group place their anonymous words in the middle of the table. Then invite each person to take one of the writings and read it during the prayer (below).

 Song: *Lord, Listen to Your Children Praying*

 Jesus says, call me, love me, know me, ask me, seek me, remember me, follow me. (Go around the circle and share what people have written.) *Jesus says, follow me, call me, love me, know me, ask me, seek me, remember me.*

Amen.

 Closing Song: *Lord, Listen to Your Children Praying*

SPIRIT FOUND IN STILLNESS

This is a simple service based on stillness and contemplation that offers a good closing to a busy day. It is based on the music of the Taizé Community and can be used with any soft meditative music.

 Have the table set with only a simple Christ candle. Have song sheets available, project music on a screen, or simply allow people to listen to the music and join in when they feel they can follow. The songs of Taizé are very simple, at most two lines long. They are repeated for a number of minutes; the songs become prayer and meditation.

The framework for the service below is open to variations. The key is to focus on simplicity and stillness, and refrain from adding too many words.

Begin in silence.

 Sing three Taizé or other simple repetitive songs or chants (see resources)

 Psalm (choose a Psalm to read or sing) *Psalm 139*

Silence (at least five minutes in length, so people can sink into the stillness)

Oh God who is the breath within our breath, the silence in our stillness, the peace at the end of our day, grant us holy rest, a deep knowing that doing nothing is a path to you, a quiet heart open to your presence, and a rested heart alive to you. Oh God who is in the space between all doing, we sit in stillness and pray.
Amen.

 Sing three Taizé or other simple repetitive songs to end.

THE CATACOMBS

This is an interesting worship to use during a confirmation class, especially if you are covering the history of the Christian Faith. It is helpful to hold the worship in a "secret" place in the church building (basement room, furnace room, bell tower, hidden attic room). It is important that youth understand the history of the faith before undertaking this service, which explores the basic ingredients of the Christian Faith: the stories we have to live by, and the practice of Communion.

 As youth arrive to the meeting have someone welcome them at the door they normally arrive at and give them these instructions: *Follow the sign of the fish and you will find the WAY. Find the way in secret.* Share no more than that with them and invite them to find their own way. Around the church grounds and rooms set out the sign of the fish, with the head of the fish pointing in the direction of the meeting.

Have the meeting room set up with a lighted Christ candle on a central table. Once all have gathered and there is stillness in the room, hold up the sign of the fish and begin.

 Welcome, Sisters and Brothers of the Way. You have found your way here through great trials and hardship. God has guided you here to this room and you are gathered with a community of believers. The task of carrying on the faith of Jesus of Nazareth has been given to us. You are one of his followers. He was on earth not so long ago and now he is gone, but the light of his life lives on in us and in his stories and message.
Christ be with you.
All: And also with you.

Share the peace of Christ with one another.

This is the time to tell the stories and to remember them so they are not forgotten. What story about Jesus can someone remember right now?

Invite suggestions, then ask the rest of the group to share what they remember about that story. Piece together the story from your collective memories. Ask prompting questions:

Didn't a boy bring Jesus the fish? How many people were there gathered there? What did Jesus do with the bread and the fish his followers brought him? How did everyone get fed? What kind of a miracle happened? Who was there? Where was the story taking place? Remember all the pieces of the story.

End the story time with these words:

We remember a story about the life of the one we follow. We share this story here tonight so we won't forget what he has brought to the world.

SHARING BREAD AND JUICE

This is another way to remember one of the last things Jesus did with his friends. He took a feast, food for the way (bread and fruit were present), and he took those foods and made them special, giving us a way to remember him and his gift in our lives. We remember the bread that he said was like his body and the juice that he said was like his blood. He asked us to eat and be fed and to remember him.

Song (see resources section)

 Somehow God, our lives have been marked with connection with your life. We give thanks for Jesus Christ, for his message of love and compassion. We understand that we are somehow connected with his life and work in this world. We have been called to be followers. Help us to pray for and remember those followers who even today must worship God in hiding, who are afraid to be who they really are in the world that they live in. We give thanks for freedom of religion and freedom to be who we really are in all ways in the world. We are blessed and we give thanks.
Amen.

 Closing Song: *Ubi Caritas* (Taizé)

FOLLOW ME

Have pieces of red string cut into lengths long enough to be tied around a person's wrist. Set the space as you wish, with a central Christ candle.

 Song: *Will You Come and Follow Me* – (John Bell and Graham Maule)

 Jesus says, follow me.
All of us have different reasons for being here tonight: maybe you came for friendship and fun, or because your parents made you come, or because you felt alone. But we all in some way have chosen to be here and to follow. Following isn't always easy. Sometimes it's hard, lonely, or weird and doesn't make sense.
So what does it mean in your life to follow?
This is a story about some people who chose to follow a long time ago.

Read Mark 1:16–20

What does following mean for you?

Invite people to share their responses with the people around them. Give time for some in-depth conversation.

Choose a song suitable for your group (see resources section)

Christians wear the symbol of a cross as a sign that they are connected to the life of Jesus. Today we offer this string to tie around your wrist as a symbol that you know you are following the path of Jesus. Take a piece of string and ask someone in the room to tie it onto your wrist. When you are tying on a string for someone, say the person's name first and then say, "You are a child of God." Think about what it means to wear this string. Think about what you will say to people if they ask about the string. You may choose to tell people about the meaning behind the string, or keep it to yourself.

Song: *Draw the Circle Wide* – (Gordon Light, *More Voices*)

Jesus, our brother and friend. We are thankful that we have freedom to follow you if we choose. We are thankful that there is a path to walk with you. We come to all the gifts, challenges, and blessings that following you brings. We draw the circle wide to include all in your love, with eyes wide open to life and to one another.
Amen.

CAMPFIRE AT NIGHT

 Have a sparkler (used on birthday cakes) for each person in the group. Have the service around a campfire in the evening, hopefully with stars and a moon overhead. If it isn't possible to be around a campfire you may wish to create a replica (indoors or out) with a number of tall pillar candles (use a variety of sizes). When grouped together the candles look very much like a campfire.

 Song: Choose a soft and inviting campfire favourite.

 Breathe in the night, all you who are gathered around this light. Breathe in the company of one another.
God who created fire, energy, and passion, we sit now in the light in awe of what surrounds us. We look up and see the night lights, the moon, and the stars. We breathe in the mystery of light so far away and feel connected. We wonder about the Holy Fire that is burning inside each person. How does the unique energy and passion of each person happen? We breathe deeply into all our wonderings.
Amen.

 Song: *This Little Light of Mine*

Light your own (leader) sparkler and allow it to burn as the group watches, then share the following questions for reflection.

 As the fire warms us, the stars guide us, and the moon hovers over us, we wonder what Holy Fire burns in your life? What part of you blazes with deep passion? How does Holy Fire touch your life?

Light another sparkler and pass the light around the circle, noticing how much light a sparkler can make. Out of darkness there comes light, over and over again.

Allow time during the closing prayer below for people to name the place where there is Holy Fire within them.

Oh God of the greater and lesser lights, we stand in awe of fire and stars and moon. We stand in awe of Light within each person, the Holy Fire that sparks creativity and life in all its fullness. Oh God, we know we have a place of deep passion within ourselves and we name those places now. (Allow random or around–the-circle sharing.) *Guide us toward Light. Guide us toward holy passion even when we think we have nothing to share. Bring us the gifts of light, and dark, and Holy Fire.*
Amen.

Sing songs around the campfire to close the evening together.

OUTDOOR PEACE VIGIL

On August 6, 1945, an atomic bomb was used on the city of Hiroshima, Japan, as an act of war on the residential population. Tens of thousands of people were killed. This service is designed to be held on August 6 (ideally outdoors at twilight), in memory of that act of war and the thousands who died, as well as to pray that peace will prevail in our world today.

If there is a place outside your church, have the vigil there, or hold it in a nearby park. Invite people from the congregation to attend. Make posters advertising the event and post them around your town. Have your youth group make peace lanterns in the weeks prior to the vigil.

On the day of the vigil, make a circle of peace lanterns (see below). Make a sign inviting people to sit in the light and pray in their own way for peace, and post it alongside the lanterns. Choose how long your vigil will be: it could be an hour or the whole evening. You may wish to have someone come into the circle every 15 minutes to share a poem or song about peace (either one they have written or someone else's). Hold silence for meditation and prayer during the remainder of each 15-minute block.

Appoint people to be in charge of watching over the lanterns, making sure no accidents happen, no lanterns are knocked over, and that candles are restocked when they burn low.

End the vigil with a closing prayer for peace that the youth have written themselves.

In Japan, there is a lantern festival where lanterns on floating bases are launched into a body of water, where they float and glow through the night. If you choose this for your vigil, please be aware that it's advisable to do so only on a calm body of water like a lake or pond and you will need to clean up the lanterns after.

© Doris Kizinna

Simple Peace Lanterns

For each lantern, decorate two pieces of plain white office paper that is thin enough to see light through and strong enough to hold form. Colour the paper or cut shapes out. Fold each paper in half horizontally, unfold, and tape the two pieces of paper together on both edges, to make a cube. You can make a round peace lantern by shaping a single piece of paper into a roll and taping the ends together. Mount the lantern onto a piece of cardboard so that it holds its form and has a base for the tea light. Add some sand to weight it down, especially if it's a windy night.

Luminaries

In Albuquerque, New Mexico, luminaries (luminaria) are traditionally placed along walkways, driveways, and even on the tops of buildings on Christmas Eve.

 For each luminary you will need a paper lunch bag, sand, and a tea light in a holder. Have youth decorate each bag with words about peace; the words will glow when the candle is lit during the vigil. Open the bag, fold over the top one inch for a nice border, fill the bag with an inch or two of sand, and place the candle inside. Place luminaries one foot apart in a circle. You could also have the luminaries form a pathway that guide people toward the vigil circle or the sign.

IN CLOSING

My prayer for you

Practice God in your life.
Speak clear deep tones of truth to all you meet.
Practice faith in many forms, and pay attention to the uncomfort-
able places you are being called.
Wonder always about your place in the Mystery.
Pray when you can, and pray even when you can't.
Keep your heart open to loving people and loving God.
The Christ is alive in you today.
Explore the cathedral of the world, and don't forget to dance.
Fall on your knees in gratitude for small things.
Pay attention, look at the stars, embrace silence, and listen for God.
The call of God in your life is expressed in how you choose to live.
The love of God in your life is expressed in how you serve.
The presence of God in your life is expressed in how you love.
Life in God, always waiting for you.
Amen.

~Doris Kizinna

a few prayers

God of Praise

God, *where everything on Earth is a prayer, we are here. To God of the invisible light between all things, we pray. We give thanks for all creation. God of the love between all things, God of touch and sorrow, expression and struggle. We give thanks to the One who brought all of this into possibility. Kindle in us the power of creation and of love, we pray. Amen.*

Found by God

You're it, God. I have sought – now it's your turn. Catch me. Show me in real ways that you are ever seeking me, even when I don't feel it. Help me feel it the moment I open my eyes. Help me feel your strong God-arms holding me. Help me to know I am always found. Amen.

God's Presence

Holy Mystery, Creator of the universe. You reveal your presence in many ways. In the earth as solid rock. In the fires of passion as spirit and light. In the waters as peace and nourishment. In the stillness as heart and call. In creation as miracle of beauty and circle of life. In mystery and possibility as presence.

Holy One, you are at work in mysterious ways. We love being at work with you in this mystery. We want to be part of shaping your world in humble and beautiful ways. Mostly, Holy One, we yearn for your presence, guiding us on. Amen.

Beginning a Youth Group Meeting

God who is our beginning, the place we all come from, the One we are like, we are gathered together to celebrate life. Gathered today are (list the names of all gathered), *children of God. We are people seeking community, your light among us, good in the world, and ways to connect with each other and the mysterious presence of you in our lives. Be with us tonight. Amen.*

Ending a Youth Group Meeting

Thanks for this place, these people, this time, this chance to live and serve together. Peace be with you until we meet again. Amen.

Love

Sweet God, you move in my life in ways I don't expect. In love between hearts. In the sweet soft movement of Spirit when two hands are clasped. In shining light between two heads bent and touching. Sweet God, you are there when the soft places are touched; when desire and time melt away, you are there. In the soft whispers and again in the sweetness of connection and friendship you are there, and I rejoice. Amen.

Light in the Dark Places

Love rescue me. Love rescue us. Bring light to the dark places. Bring joy to the dark places. Rescue us from fear; surround us with joy. Amen.

Resources

Youth Specific Books

Mark Yaconelli, *Contemplative Youth Ministry: Practicing the Presence of Jesus* (Grand Rapids, MI: Zondervan, 2006)

Kenda Creasy Dean and Ron Foster, *The Godbearing Life: The Art of Soul-Tending for Youth Ministry* (Nashville: Upper Room Books, 1998)

Dorothy C. Bass & Don C. Richter, *Way to Live: Christian Practices for Teens* (Nashville: Upper Room Books, 2002)

Sarah Arthur, *The God Hungry Imagination: The Art of Storytelling for Postmodern Youth Ministry* (Nashville: Upper Room Books, 2007)

General Books

Parker J. Palmer, *The Active Life: A Spirituality of Work, Creativity and Caring* (San Francisco: Jossey-Bass, 1999)

Rob Bell, *Velvet Elvis: Repainting the Christian Faith* (Grand Rapids, MI: Zondervan, 2005)

Marcus Borg, *The Heart of Christianity* (San Francisco: Harper San Francisco, 2003) and the two study guides to accompany this book:
(1) Tim Scorer, *Experiencing the Heart of Christianity*, (Kelowna, BC: Wood Lake Publishing, 2005) and
(2) Marcus Borg and Tim Scorer, *Living the Heart of Christianity* (Kelowna, BC: Wood Lake Publishing, 2004)

Wayne W. Dyer, *The Power of Intention: Learning to Co-Create Your World Your Way* (Carson, CA: Hay House, 2004)

Kathryn Spink, *A Universal Heart: The Life and Vision of Brother Roger of Taizé* (Chicago: GIA Publications, 2006)

Jacques Berthier, *Songs & Prayers from Taizé* (Chicago: GIA Publications, 1994)

Shane Claiborne, *The Irresistible Revolution: Living as an Ordinary Radical* (Grand Rapids, MI: Zondervan, 2006)

Parker J. Palmer, *Let Your Life Speak: Listening for the Voice of Vocation* (San Francisco: Jossey-Bass, 2000)

Richard Louv, *Last Child in the Woods* (Chapel Hill, NC: Algonquin Books of Chapel Hill, 2005)

Peter Menzel, *Hungry Planet: What the World Eats* (Berkeley, CA: Material World Books/Ten Speed Press, 2005)

Jean McMann, *Altars & Icons: Sacred Spaces in Everyday Life* (San Francisco: Chronicle Books, 1998)

Sam M. Intrator & Megan Scribner, *Leading from Within: Poetry that Sustains the Courage to Lead* (San Francisco: Jossey-Bass, 2007)

Marcus Braybrooke, *1000 World Prayers* (Oakland, CA: O Books, 2003)

Related to the Practices

Roger Joslin, *Running the Spiritual Path* (New York: Griffin, 2004)

Dorothy C. Bass, ed., *Practicing Our Faith: A Way of Life for a Searching People* (San Francisco: Jossey-Bass, 1998)

Stephanie Paulsell, *Honoring the Body: Meditations on a Christian Practice* (San Francisco: Jossey-Bass, 2002)

Dorothy C. Bass, *Receiving the Day: Christian Practices for Opening the Gift of Time* (San Francisco: Jossey-Bass, 2001)

Joanna R. Macy and Molly Young Brown, *Coming Back to Life: Practices to Reconnect Our Lives, Our World* (Philadelphia: New Society Publishers, 1998)

Alice Peck, *Bread, Body, Spirit: Finding the Sacred in Food* (Woodstock, VT: Skylight Paths, 2008)

Seena B. Frost, *Soul Collage* (Santa Cruz, CA: Hanford Mead Publisher Inc., 2001)

Mary Anne McFarlane & E. Ann Flemming, *Arts and the Spirit* (Toronto, ON: United Church Publishing House, 2007)

Tara Jon Manning, *Mindful Knitting* (North Clarendon, VT: Tuttle Publishing, 2004)

Susan S. Jorgensen and Susan S. Izard, *Knitting into the Mystery: A Guide to the Shawl Knitting Ministry* (Ridgefield, CT: Morehouse Publishing 2003)

Monique Mandali, *Mandala Coloring Books, Volumes 1–4* (Helena, MN: Mandali Publishing, 1977–2000)

Neil Paynter, *Blessed Be Our Table: Graces for Mealtimes and Reflections on Food* (Glasgow: Wild Goose Publishing, 2003)

Children's Books

Douglas Wood, *Old Turtle* (New York: Scholastic Press, 1992)

Douglas Wood, *Old Turtle and the Broken Truth* (New York: Scholastic Press 2003)

Colin Thompson and Amy Lissiat, *The Short and Incredibly Happy Life of Riley* (Brooklyn: Kane Miller Book Publishers, 2007)

Shaun Tan, *The Red Tree* (Vancouver, BC: Simply Read Books, 2003)

Daniel Manus Pinkwater, *The Big Orange Splot* (New York: Scholastic Press, 1993)

Sarah S. Kilborne, *Peach and Blue* (Toronto, ON: Random House Canada, 1994)

Byrd Baylor, *The Way to Start the Day* (Palmer, AK: Aladdin Paperbacks, 1977)

Sandy Eisenberg Sasso, *In God's Name* (Woodstock, VT: Jewish Lights Publishing, 1994)

Nicholas Allan, *Jesus' Day Off* (New York: Random House, 1998)

Music Books

More Voices (Toronto: United Church Publishing House, and Kelowna, BC: Wood Lake Publishing, 2007)

Recorded Music

The Prayer Cycle, Jonathan Elias (composer) (Sony Classical Records, 1999)

Songs and Prayers of Taizé, GIA Publications, 1995

The 23rd Psalm, Bobby McFerrin, from the album Medicine Music 1998

Gregorian Chants, Officium Jan Gabarek & The Hilliard Ensemble, ECM Records, 1994

Websites and Other Resources

retreatsonline.com listing of retreat locations worldwide

taize.org website for the Taizé community in France

veriditas.labyrinthsociety.org directory of labyrinths worldwide and labyrinth resources

rottentomatoes.com: for movie reviews and ideas

alternativeworship.org alternative worship resources and services worldwide

practicingourfaith.org series of resources on practicing the Christian faith

waytolive.org related to the book *Way to Live* (Christian practices for teens)

spiritualityandpractice.com variety of practices from various traditions

catholicireland.net/talk2god children's prayer practice

www.yfc.co.uk/labyrinth/online online labyrinth

www.worldprayers.org thousands of prayers from around the world

iona.org.uk ecumenical Christian community in Scotland

naramatacentre.net United Church retreat and conference centre